Shirley Thom

MW00760882

LIFE
IS A
SALES JOB

Everyone sells.
You might as well
do it right and
be handsomely
rewarded.

S H I R L E Y   T H O M

Seattle, Washington
Portland, Oregon
Denver, Colorado
Vancouver, B.C.
Scottsdale, Arizona

Copyright © 1999 Shirley Thom

All rights reserved. Except for use in a review, the repro-
duction or use of work in any form by any electronic,
mechanical, or other means now known or invented here-
after, including xerography, photocopying, recording,
information storage and retrieval systems, is forbidden
without the written permission of the publisher.

Manufactured in the United States of America.
Cover Design by David Marty
Interior by Gopa Design

LCCCN: 98-067842
ISBN: 0-89716-852-6

Published by Peanut Butter Publishing
Pier 55, 1101 Alaskan Way, Suite 301
Seattle, WA 98101-2982
206-748-0345 • e-mail: pnutpub@aol.com
http://www.pbpublishing.com
Denver, Colorado • Scottsdale, Arizona
Portland, Oregon • Milwaukee, Wisconsin
Minneapolis/St.Paul, Minnesota
Chicago, Illinois • Vancouver, BC

Contents

CONTENTS

A Few Words from the Author

THIS BOOK IS WRITTEN for the person who has not yet decided on a career, the professional wayfarer still searching for just the right profitable passion to follow. The key word here is profitable. I always thought I'd like to paint for a living. It was something I loved to do. Why not make money doing something I love? That's the ultimate dream, after all. But posthumous biographies of my favorite artists were so often filled with adjectives such as "poor" and "starving," I decided I would just paint on weekends and give my paintings to people who may like them. My dreams included a number of creature comforts that only money could buy.

This book is also written for the person who has already chosen a career in sales as a seller and/or manager, who would like to find more consistent and less stressful ways to achieve goals and increase personal income. I chose broadcast sales as a career and discovered an attitudinal approach to selling that has allowed me to thrive in a professional field notorious for its stress and burnout.

I was plugging away in a clerical position at a radio station, living paycheck to paycheck, thinking this was a long way from the passion and profit I'd dreamed I would be enjoying. Still looking for career options, I noticed that the people around me who appeared to be having the most fun and making the most money were working in the sales department. I asked myself, why not go there? They seem to have something I think I'm missing. For two years I focused my mind and energy toward getting myself into a position in sales. Focus, when it's well managed, will get you anything.

That was more than twenty years ago. I'm still focused and selling, and still having fun and making money. The secret to my longevity in sales is that I do nothing in my sales career that I don't do in the rest of my life. I approach my sales goals in the same way as I pursue my life ambitions, with a combination of holism and practicality. The focus is on personal motivation and discipline. It has to be personal. I am the only person who truly understands the source of my motivation, and therefore the only person who can determine what I'm willing to do to realize the fulfillment of what motivates me. It's my life and I'll decide how I'm going to live it.

Sales is not difficult. It's a natural profession. Everyone sells. Every waking moment, from the day we are born, trying to get food into our bellies the instant we know we're hungry, to our last day on earth, trying to negotiate a few more minutes, and perhaps even beyond, posturing ourselves at the pearly gates, we sell. We can't not sell. Life is a Sales Job. We might as well get paid for it.

Endorsements

"Like having Willie Mays as your Little League coach, or learning times tables from Pythagoras, I have been so fortunate to have learned from the very best since the beginning of my media sales career. Over the years Shirley has become a trusted friend and an invaluable mentor. I am thrilled that so many people will now have the opportunity to learn, as I have, from the wit and wisdom of Shirley Thom."
                                    Rob Leydon, Account Executive
                                    TCI Media Services, Seattle, WA

"People ask me, 'Just what is it about Shirley Thom?' I tell them she's the toughest sales manager I ever had. I also tell them she's made me more money than any sales manager I ever had."
                                    Jim Stofer, Western Regional Manager
                                    Strata Marketing, Issaquah, WA

"Shirley doesn't play political games or engage in office chit chat. That makes some people nervous. They don't understand how focused she is. If I had to use one word to describe her work temperament, it would be focus. Her eye is always on the finish line."
                                    Tyrone Noble, Principle
                                    New Media Communications, Seattle, WA

"If you've lost perspective and are letting your work control you, Shirley makes you take a break. She insists that you balance your life."
                                    Regan Cole, Media Sales Consultant
                                    Chicago, IL

"Shirley is tough. She expects excellence. But you know she cares, so you give it to her. She makes you believe in yourself."

Michael Alhadeff, Account Executive
KOMO Radio, Seattle, WA

"Shirley taught me how to communicate and build relationships at each level of the sales process. I learned that sales is a part of our lives, everyday. She was instrumental in helping me turn my personal skills into sales results."

Anita Murrmann, Senior Marketing Manager
Meredith Corporation, Chicago, IL

"Shirley's techniques helped me to focus on the big picture, reduce stress, and handle my relationships with more grace. Under her management I tripled my income in 3 years."

Michelle Cody, Account Executive
KMTT Radio, Seattle, WA

Shirley is great at sizing up the situation and the person, and evaluating how their personal and professional needs will fit. She's persistent, but she never forces a sale until she finds a way to make it work for everyone. She wants lifetime clients."

Cindy Fox, Asst. Athletic Director
Kansas State University, Manhattan, KA

"When Shirley was my client, 'raising the bar' was a daily exercise that I pushed myself and the firm to exceed. Shirley's inspiring desire to win brings out the same desire in others."

Darren McMillan, Account Executive
KYCY Radio, San Francisco, CA

"Shirley gives credence to the axiom that ordinary people willing to put forth extraordinary effort can accomplish their goals and live their dreams."
Cheryl Stewart, Account Executive
KING 5 Television, Seattle, WA

"When she was coaching me she always said, 'Keep your eye on the ball and follow through.' And it worked."

Alex Suryan, Shortstop
MTYAA Pony League, Mountlake Terrace, WA

Personal Acknowledgements

Rebecca Lee Suryan and Shannon Jean Archer.
Did I raise them or did they raise me?
Without them, little. With them, everything.

Texanna Thompson Casey
Flower girl, cousin, confidante

Penny Smith
Courageous life explorer, sister

Taylor Hayes, Rita Gilfelen, Judith Strand.
Definition of friends

Susan Dingethal
Indescribable, but "there"

Professional Acknowledgements

Fred Kaufman. My first sales manager, my mentor.
Without the example of his integrity I would not have
considered sales as a career, and I would have missed
out on a very satisfying aspect of my life.

Richard Kale. My teacher, my disciplinarian.
Richard taught me the value of setting goals and having
an action plan. Without him I'd still be wandering around,
wondering what to do next.

Nick Lacy. The most skilled sales person I know.
I was his apprentice, his colleague, his sales manager.
But Nick needed no sales manager.
He relishes the art of the sale. Many of his
techniques are incorporated in this book.

Larry Coffman. My first publisher.
For whatever reason, he believed in
my writing skills enough to print a few articles
with my name attached to them.
It's his fault I caught the writing bug.

Dedication

Robert L. Scott
Your unconditional personal and professional
support carried me through days of joy and doubt.
How dare you leave me now.

CHAPTER ONE

Wake Up
With An Attitude

"Don't confuse having a career with having a life.
They are not the same."

Hillary Rodham Clinton,
1998 Commencement Address, Howard University

IT'S MORNING. You open your eyes and look around. You see the rain pounding against the window and you remember you left your umbrella at the office. Or you gratefully thank the rain clouds for nourishing the newly-planted grass seed. Your ears awaken too, and you hear the welcome sound of birds singing. Or you hear the irritating noise of the neighbor's dog barking, AGAIN.

You nudge the person lying next to you and he rolls over. You notice the drool running down his chin, and you move away. Or you see the sweet, bleary-eyed morning grin, and you move a little closer.

How do you want to start your day? What you see and hear is not what you get. It's what you make of it. Are you going to see the slobber or the smile?

You've only been awake a few seconds and you are already manipulating the facts. You're selling yourself on the product of this day, and by the way, the look your partner sees on your face is going to be selling him at close range too. How do you want him to respond to your first encounter? Now is the time for you to either close the deal or leave it hanging for another, more perfect day. Close the deal right now, and you can count on a day full of successful responses. Let it go and you may lose your sale forever. A perfect day may never come along by itself. The world is full of barking dogs, if you choose to hear them. Or you can listen to the sounds of singing birds. You're the salesperson, and it's your life. You decide.

I am a professional salesperson, and I like what I do for a living. I like it because I live it. And because I'm a salesperson, I do begin to manipulate the facts of the day the instant I wake up, because I can mold the product of this day to fit my own program. My best days come from mornings when I awaken early and have time to lie in bed a while and remind myself of the choices I have. Like today, for instance.

This is the 87th day in a row that I see nothing but dark clouds when I open my eyes. It's the 8th day of June and I'm fed up with these dark Seattle days. I'm going to be crabby today because I'm fed up with the rain, and I'm going to make sure everyone around me is crabby and fed up too. I'm not going to be crabby and fed up by myself. I'll set my mood right now, with a sigh or two. (Sigh, sigh....) There. It's starting.

What shall I wear? It has to be something crabby. I know just the outfit. I'll put on that ugly green jersey dress I bought on sale last November. An ugly November dress in June. That ought to shore up the crabbiness. Then what? Then I'll go into the office and work on budgets. Perfect. Today I'm going to work on budgets in my ugly green dress and hold my head down and grumble, because it's raining and I'm mad.

Uh-oh. I have an 11:00 appointment with Jolly George. Damn! I can't be crabby with Jolly George. George has money to spend, and I want him to spend at least some of it with me. But Jolly George won't spend money with a crab in an ugly green dress. Let's try this awakening scene again. (Sigh....) That will be my last sigh of the day.

Will you look at that cloud formation! It looks like a big, fluffy dog paddling across the sky. Let's see. What's up for today...? Right. I have an 11:00 meeting with George Smith.

You know, I've put together a pretty good plan for his late summer promotion. If I get out of bed right now, I'll have time to rehearse it one more time before our meeting. I'll wear that new salmon-colored suit I bought in anticipation of warm summer days. Great color! Maybe George will have time for lunch after the presentation. He's such a pleasant man. What am I waiting for? Time to get up and go make myself some money.

Which scene do you think will bring a greater return on investment for my time and energy?

If I weren't working in commissioned sales, I would let the day dictate my mood. I'd go with the flow and let life happen to me. Dark clouds? Crabby day. Sunshine? Smiley day. And since I'm a Seattle native, which otherwise is a lovely place to live, my ratio of days crabby to days smiley would be about 3-to-1, in favor of crabby.

Weather is not the only factor that could have an effect on my daily mood, but it's a perfect excuse, because it's something I can do nothing about. It isn't my fault the sun doesn't come out to greet me. It's the sun's fault. I can't help it if I bought an ugly dress. The store marked it down to make me buy it. And if I were to continue with this attitude? It's not my fault that stupid George won't buy advertising on my radio station. Our ratings aren't what they used to be. His ads probably wouldn't work anyway. How am I going to increase my billing if the radio station keeps slipping in the ratings books? It's not my fault.

Lucky for me, life took a turn to push me into a career in sales and it taught me to not get caught up in these "not my fault" excuses. It doesn't matter whose fault it is. It doesn't matter if it's raining or the dress is dumb or if that damn dog's yapping wakes me up every morning. All that matters is my attitude toward these irritants. They are not going to control my life. I am.

The turn that saved me was a divorce. Out of adversity come many positive things, right? Suddenly I was single with two daughters, ages five and eight, to take care of on my own, with little where-withal to figure out what to do or how to do it. In the divorce I got the house, which meant I also got the house payments. I needed money. I needed a job, but I hadn't been a part of the work force for eight years. What on earth was I going to do? To start with, I called on people I knew. Perfect place to start.

Friends in the broadcast industry found me a clerical position at a radio station, where I could put my limited secretarial skills to use. It was a good place to begin, but I soon found that clerical jobs pay only enough to barely cover the monthly bills. They don't offer enough to pay for new adventures or guarantee financial security. I decided my girls and I deserved more than just the rudiments of basic living.

I looked around the radio station to see what other people were doing to earn their daily bread. I looked at disc jockeys and news people. They had beautiful voices, and they spent a lot of time complaining about not having enough money to pay their bills. I was sure they were making more money than I was, but I didn't want to change jobs just to make a *little* more money. Besides, there were no dulcet tones hiding in my vocal chords waiting to be discovered.

Well how about those sales people? They were always laughing and coming and going whenever they wanted to, and telling us about the fun lunches they were having. And they made money—lots of money. Observing their behavior, I thought I could do what they were doing. They didn't seem to have any particular talents, except for the ability to talk and laugh a lot. I could teach myself to talk more, and if I made more money I knew I would laugh a lot more.

Having decided to "do" sales, I spent two years listening to what the sales people said, studying their proposals, and getting to know their clients' needs and habits. Two years may seem like a lengthy period of time in today's speedy, move-into-high-gear-as-fast-as-you-can world. But I was teaching myself, and I wanted to be absolutely certain I would do it right when I got the chance. If this effort panned out, it would make me the first rookie and first woman to work in sales for this company.

The chance came with the posting of a new opening in the sales department.

Fisher Broadcasting Inc. is a solid, conservative company, and, like most other distinguished companies, not necessarily inclined to establish firsts of any kind. But rookie and woman factors aside, I figured there were other things going on that might not come together again soon. It was time for me to make a move.

1. I needed more personal income.

2. The opportunity to fill the need presented itself.

3. My preparation had put me in a position to take advantage of the opportunity.

4. The timing was right for equal opportunity.

I approached Fred Kaufman, General Sales Manager for KOMO Radio. I told him I would like to be considered for the new sales position.

"I was wondering if you were going to make a move," he said. "Let's talk."

We met and I presented the case for my joining his sales team, citing my two years of preparation.

"I've been watching you and I thought we'd be having this talk," he said. "The position we're offering is a new position. People seldom leave here. We don't have openings very often. But our business is changing and we need new people who might bring us a new idea or two. We were hoping someone like you would apply. We'll teach you the ground rules of how we do business and give you plenty of time to develop your skills. *We're in this for the long haul.* I'm sure you'll do well. Let's try it."

I had just made my first sale without even realizing I was involved in a sale. I thought it was simply a matter of perfect timing where my needs happened to match up with theirs. Today, when I review how this presentation took place, I realize that the primary reason the sale went through was that all the classic conditions for putting together a successful transaction were present:

NEED
OPPORTUNITY
PREPARATION
TIMING

It's never just timing. It's these four criteria arriving together that brings about the probability of a sale. Whether we are making a decision to marry, purchase a home, launch a new career, or go on a single sales call, we must sit ourselves down and test the presence of all four of these key conditions before we waste needless time preparing to fill a need that doesn't exist, or take advantage of an opportunity whose time has not yet come.

This is a reflective observation of a sale that took place more than twenty years ago. It's a valid observation based on experience. My immediate reaction, however, had far greater impact on the growth of my career and my life than all the knowledge and experience I've acquired since that time.

Fred Kaufman hired me for two reasons. He had noticed the work I'd done over a two-year period, and he believed the presentation I had just given him. In preparing for this opportunity, I'd forgotten to take on the personality of the sales team I'd been observing. I became so focused on what I needed to do and how I wanted to do it that it never occurred to me to either embellish my qualifications or beef up my act. I presented myself, and Fred Kaufman hired me. No shticks, no tricks, no sleaze. With relief, I discovered that the career path I'd chosen would not require me to change either my persona or my personal convictions. I had done nothing to close the sale that I wouldn't do in any aspect of my life, to get something I truly wanted.

Some people shy away from sales because they're convinced it takes a laughing, lunching, fast-talking, insincere kind of personality to be successful, and they don't want to be that kind of person. People who believe this myth are mistaken about what it takes to be successful in sales. The integrity of the very successful man who accepted my first sales proposal and welcomed me into the professional sales arena changed my attitude on this issue.

Some people go into sales because they also believe it takes that kind of personality, and they think they can shag it. Rather than adjust to honest dedication and hard work when the con games fail to produce long-term results, they keep the career fable alive and change jobs in search of another rainmaker's promise of riches. These people don't understand the ethics of sales any more than those who choose not to enter the profession in the first place.

Those who stay away from sales, and those who eventually leave, believe that a career in sales requires them to take on a repertoire of behaviors outside their personal values, somewhere on the fringe of acceptable society. They believe, as I once did, that sales is not a serious career. They perceive it to be a short-term, notice-me scheme to enter the money game. They view sales as a necessary building block to a real profession. To be noticed and promoted, they think they have to work the sales game by moving fast and making a lot of noise, even if it is unnatural.

Being fast and noisy works for some products in certain business environments. There are people who are genuinely loud, gregarious, back slapping self-promoters who can work in those places and become very good sellers for the products they offer. I get a kick out of these people and take my hat off to them. But people like me, who don't have these overt characteristics, can also have excellent sales careers. We don't have to adopt personalities and habits that belong to someone else. There are enough sales careers to go around. Be yourself. *What works is what's real.*

Unfortunately, the extroverts almost always get the first nod when a sales position is available. No matter what kind of personal qualifications the product type would seem to require, employers are caught up in the sales hyperbole. They've heard and read about sales successes, all of which seem to have occurred as a result of overt, aggressive behavior. As a result, they may believe that all products are sold the same way, or they know their product may be different from the successes they hear about, but they don't want to risk a new approach. During the interview process they set up scenarios to see how fast the applicants can snap, crackle, and pop. They are searching for the Rice Crispy Rep of radio advertising, aluminum siding, hosiery, mufflers, or bakery sales. And what do they get?

They get exactly what they were looking for, and if the product does not fit the profile, they will be looking for a new sales representative sooner than they expected. The crackling crispy rep they hired will not deliver the sales that either one of them had hoped for. The frustrating and expensive process of sales employee turnover will take place again.

More than eighty percent of new commissioned sales positions turn over in less than eighteen months. I've interviewed enough managers looking for sellers to be surprised the percentage isn't higher. I can't believe how bullheaded and single-minded managers are in continuing to act on preconceived notions that continue to prove themselves wrong.

Bad hiring decisions affect more than the company making the hiring mistakes. The single, most prevalent complaint I hear from clients is the number of *different* sales representatives they work with per company. Just as they are about to get their new reps trained to act like normal human beings delivering information they asked for, the person they've trained is gone and they have to train someone new. Clients shouldn't have to train their sales representatives. The right sales people should be hired in the first place.

The sad fact is that most of the people looking for positions in sales are capable of acceptable behavior and really are quite pleasant to be around outside the workplace. But the perception they get from the people filling the positions they apply for is that they have to act goofy to get the job. When people feel they are forced to develop a second personality in an attempt to acquire perceived assets in the business world, they lose their sense of self. They also lose their ability to recognize what works for them and what doesn't. Success eludes them and they become disenchanted.

Some people figure out the source of their failures and conflict, and drop their alter ego. Far more people keep up this charade their entire lives, keeping the second persona around to throw into the interview ring and win jobs they don't like and can't do. Once you're hired on the basis of what your second face revealed, you're stuck with it. I can't imagine a more frustrating and exhausting burden than trying to coordinate the wearing of two faces, one face for the business world and one for your personal life, when one face will do. The face you show yourself when you first wake up is the only face you'll ever need. Get to know that face and stay with it. Answer to the master in the morning mirror and you'll have fewer problems answering to the rest of the world.

Raise Your Right Hand and Take this Oath:

I've come to terms with my own values and priorities.

I will be the same person at work as I am at home.

I will work only with people who accept my personal style as well as my skills.

This does not mean that my supervisors, colleagues, clients, and I are going to be twenty-four hour buddies who will always agree. It means that while we may disagree on issues, we will respect each other's values and resolve issues like the adults we claim to be. It also means that I can take myself to work and bring myself home, wearing the same face. It may not be the greatest face in the world, but it's mine and it works for me.

Will self-integration guarantee success? My definition of success is this:

Success is a process requiring the right combination of talent, skill, and luck to give you the opportunity to achieve what you want.

There are no guarantees in a process. I can guarantee, however, that self-integration will make the process less stressful and there-fore more likely to bring favorable results.

The Goal of Sales Is Results

1. Results are **measurable**.

2. Results require a **plan**.

3. Results are measured **at the end of each day**.

Before you go to bed each night, take a few moments to reflect on the day you've just lived. Ask yourself three questions:

1. Was it a good day?

2. What made it good?

3. What did I do to make it good?

Answer them and be done with it. This day is over. Sleep well. Tomorrow you will get another chance to have a good day.

It's morning again, and it's raining. Glorious, wet, wonderful rain is tap, tap, tapping at my windowsill. It's not the kind of weather I would have chosen for this day, but it's what I've been handed by the Weather God, and I am going to work with it.

✦ There is someone next to me expecting a morning smile, and I want to give it.

✦ There is a client waiting for me downtown expecting a killer presentation, and I want to do it.

✦ There are colleagues at work expecting a plan and a few words of wisdom, and I want them to receive them.

✦ There are friends meeting me at the ballpark after work expecting to have a good time, and I want us to have it.

This new day has a number of wins waiting to happen, if I can just get myself out of bed with a positive attitude. Feet! Hit the floor!

We have work to do.

CHAPTER TWO

Why Sell?

You already do. Everybody sells. You may as well do it right
and be handsomely rewarded for your efforts.

I'VE WRITTEN THAT SOME PEOPLE shy away from sales and some people leave sales. If this were true, it would appear that some people are not selling. So what is this "everybody sells" declaration? There's no need to look for contradiction. Everybody does sell. Some get paid for it and some don't. It's getting paid for it that seems to make people nervous, and I'm not sure why. Perhaps it comes from centuries of feelings about rewarding the world's oldest professions.

Everybody makes love; everybody gives advice; everybody borrows money; everybody sells. Can you say prostitute, attorney, loan shark, and salesperson all in one sentence? I guess most people don't care to admit that they do these things for money. Let's try to move the salesperson up a notch in the socially acceptable hierarchy. The others will have to take care of their own reputations.

Sales is hard work, requiring years of preparation and practice, just like any worthwhile profession. There are no shortcuts to a rewarding sales career. The minimum time investment to reach the point of feeling comfortable with your career in sales and reaping a steady income from it is two years. And that's if you're starting with industry knowledge, an attentive mentor, and a great deal of self-esteem. The quick, easy sale will occasionally come along to pick you up after weeks of banging your head on the brick wall of rejection. But the easy sale is just a tease to keep you from giving up prematurely. Two years won't put you in the big leagues, but it will get you established into a comfortable income until you get the call up. And it will give you enough time to decide if commissioned sales is the career you want. Is a career in sales worth a two-year investment?

You could take a comfortable job with a steady income from the get-go. Any number of jobs will pay the rent without putting you in the uncomfortable position of having to ask a stranger for money. Why not just pay the rent and pass through life content to be handed whatever wages your employer sees fit to give you? Most likely you will keep up with the cost of living, and at age sixty you will have as much as you had when you were twenty-five, relative to the market economy. No waiting, no highs, no lows, no discomfort.

There is nothing wrong with living this kind of steady, comfortable life. But, I've never known anyone who's chosen such a life to wish the same for his or her children. We dream of more for our next generations. Why not dream of more for ourselves?

I'm not claiming that sales is the ultimate career choice and everyone should do it. People who have a specific passion, in science, law, the arts, teaching, homemaking, or whatever, should follow their passion as far as it takes them. What I'm suggesting, however, is that sales is a career equal to any other in satisfaction and growth potential, and it may offer advantages over other careers for some people.

Before we explore the many reasons to choose a career in sales, I need to qualify that this is all about **commissioned sales**. The commission part is both the advantage and the challenge that sets it apart from other career options. Commissioned sales is different from other professions in that compensation is based solely on measured results. There is no hourly wage or monthly salary. What you earn is directly related to what you've accomplished. No sales = no income. No results = no money. Commissioned sales-people are paid for results. It's not for the faint of heart. It's only for people who **believe** in themselves and have the **courage** to put that belief on the line.

Commissioned Sales Is Not a Salaried Job

✦ Initially, you may make less money than if you took a salaried position in your chosen field of interest.

✦ Like any profession with growth potential, it will take more than 40 hours a week to build a client base and increase your income.

✦ You are solely responsible for your income. After a standard six-month "guarantee," whatever you make will depend on how much you sell.

✦ The company you work for will keep 80–90% of every dollar you bring to it. That may seem like a high percentage that does not end up in your pockets, but the company's expenses are higher than yours.

✦ You are always in the middle of the responsibility chain. The client's responsibility buck stops with you. You are the only person he knows, or wants to know, who can get the job done. No production excuses allowed. Your supervisor's responsibility buck stops with you. The revenue flow starts with you. You are the resource for his favorable or unfavorable fiscal reports.

✦ There are no plateaus. What you did last year or last month does not matter. Your dues are never paid in full. Your entire career will be based on your inclination and ability to produce more, more, more.

✦ You have little, if any, influence over the performance or marketing of the product you are selling. Regardless of what happens with the product in the world of supply and demand and marketplace competition, you must sell it at a price that will assure the company's projected sales figures.

✦ You are going to lose more sales than you win. Accepting daily losses takes some getting used to. Until you learn to depersonalize the losses, your self-esteem could take quite a hit. You need to start your career with a lot of belief in what you can deliver. But it is important to recognize the possibility of some slippage and to maintain a support system that will help you hold on until more wins come your way.

Have I scared you away yet? It has always been my style to search out the negatives, put them on the table, take care of them one by one, and then move forward, full steam ahead, green lights all the way. And now that we've eaten all our vegetables, the rest is dessert. Why would you want to earn a living in commissioned sales?

1. Every product and service needs to be sold. There will *always* be sales positions available.

2. Sales careers can cross product lines. You can go with whatever you find to be new and interesting. Teachers cannot become news writers, writers cannot become dance choreographers, and dancers cannot become medical doctors, just because they have taken an interest in a new field. They would have to make significant changes in their lifestyles and invest a considerable amount of time to change careers. A salesperson can sell textbooks, newspaper advertising, season tickets to the ballet, or pharmaceutical products, with two weeks' notice in his or her current position. I'm not an advocate of job-hopping, but when a career needs refreshing, sales careers are more easily freshened than others.

3. Every sale is an affirmation of your success. You won't need to wait for quarterly reports or your supervisor's feedback to know you are doing a good job. You will know after each successful transaction.

4. Commissioned sales is lucrative. You can consistently increase your income without having to ask for a raise. Eventually you will make more money than in a typical salaried position...a *lot* more money.

5. Commissioned sales allows you to change your wish list into a to do list. In a salaried position you can wish for a new car this fall or a luxury vacation next summer. If your current income allows for these wishes to come true, go out and buy them. If not, you can ask for a raise. Based on what? You can tap into your savings. What about the rainy day? You can cut expenses in another area. And still, you may not get your wishes in your desired time frame.

   In commissioned sales, you figure the cost of your wish, figure what you must sell to cover the cost, and go after it. You don't have to ask anyone for permission to make more money. You leave your savings in the bank and continue with your current budget. Junior doesn't have to sacrifice his guitar lessons so you can buy your sports car. In commissioned sales extra effort not only counts, it pays.

6. In commissioned sales you choose the people you work with. Certain people are attracted to certain industries. Set aside time to visit selected work environments and observe the people who work there. Spend a day on Wall Street, or an hour in a Microsoft cafeteria, or observe the staff's interaction with customers at Wendy's or Nordstrom. Ask questions of the people who work there — the people on the front line, not in the Boardroom. People are the single most valuable asset in the workplace. You can sell anything. Are the people you observe the kind of people you want to hang out with?

7. Commissioned sales allows you to choose the hours when you do your best work. All of us have our biological energy clocks. If you prefer quiet time in the morning, bury your head in paperwork until you're feeling more sociable. If you need a challenge to get the day started, schedule a power breakfast with your most important client. There is enough variety in your sales day to allow you to allocate your energy levels toward a specific task at your best time to get it done.

8. Commissioned sales is the door most often opened to career advancement. Selling requires all-encompassing product knowledge. Sales professionals know as much about the company as anyone on staff. Courage, belief, and self-motivation are traits deemed necessary for a career in sales, the same qualities sought in putting together management teams. Proven results are evident. It's hard to argue with documented results.

9. Commissioned sales requires you to constantly learn and grow. Sales is an active profession. You must listen and communicate; you must keep up with industry changes and challenges; you must keep up with clients' changing needs; you must create new ideas and make them saleable; you must initiate action and actively react. You learn, you create, you work, and you grow. What could be more exciting than a lifetime of knowledge and growth?

10. Sales demands a better physical presentation. Bright eyes, good posture, and clear thinking call for a healthy lifestyle. Would anyone really mourn the disappearance of ratty ponytails?

11. Sales demands better verbal presentations. Think of the time we'd save if we were to eliminate the "ums" and "you knows" from our conversations. Faces might miraculously appear from behind newspapers at the breakfast table.

12. Sales skills are useful away from work. You will learn to antic-

ipate the needs of your family and friends with the same perceptions you've learned to apply to the needs of your clients.
You'll be more empathetic. Here's an example I could cite mul-
tiple times from personal experience and observation. A client
has been involved in a fender bender. You offer unconditional
support. "How are you ... can I help...do you need a ride?" Your
client says, "My husband is just going to kill me. I'm in real
trouble now." If it were your wife or husband in the accident,
would your first question be the same as for your client, or
would it be, "Whose fault was it?" Would your family be afraid
of your response, or could they count on the same support you
give your clients? Learn to apply the same considerations to
people at home as you do at work.

13. Sales is as much about emotion as money. You will be unable
to stifle all the highs and lows. Sales takes away the burden of
emotional reticence.

14. Last, and certainly not least, salespeople are some of the most
terrific people you will ever know. Your colleagues will exhib-
it all the wonderful traits that excellent sales people have. You
will see their Courage, Commitment, Empathy, Communication Skills, Sharp Minds, High Self-Esteem, Sense of Humor,
and many more wonderful traits. The skills and talents of excellent salespeople are as varied as the number of salespeople.
Your colleagues will support your efforts when you need support and kick your butt when it needs kicking. They will be
there for you today and all your days to come.

Salespeople really are the laughing good-time Charlies I imagined them to be when I looked around the radio station twenty
years ago to see what kind of career I might like to pursue, and
thank goodness for that. Yet they are a whole lot more. Being a part
of a sales team is the closest thing I can think of to being a part of
the psychedelic lineup of a baseball team, and it just doesn't get
any better than that.

In commissioned sales you will make as much money as you want, doing work you like with people you like, at a time of day you do your best work, learning and growing as you perform, creating better atmospheres and opportunities for yourself, personally as well as professionally. It's not a bad career choice. I'd do it myself.

You sell yourself every day to yourself, your family, your friends, and your colleagues. The product you sell is yourself. You may as well become acutely conscious of who you are and use your self-knowledge to develop your assets and reap measurable returns.

CHAPTER THREE

Your Mirror Image

The only product you really sell is yourself, and the most important product feature you have is your mirror image.

YOU ARE PERPETUALLY ON STAGE, selling yourself to everyone you encounter, including yourself. The first and most important product you sell is your **Mirror Image**. Your appearance is the first thing people notice about you, and it will create the first impression of the rest of you. It is nearly impossible to overcome a bad first impression.

Like it or not, we are judged instantly by our physical appearance. We can get all huffy about the injustice of it all, but the fact is we can't escape how we look and it does matter, so let's make sure we understand the implications of our physical realities and see if we want to do anything about what they reflect.

Taking a close, honest look at our own reflection can be disconcerting. We may not like everything the mirror reflects, but we need to see ourselves as others see us. Their eyes don't know what we *want* them to see. They don't give us more hair or subtract twenty pounds.

Can you tell the truth about your physical appearance? When you stroll past that full-length mirror in your private dressing area, do you suck in the gut a little and pretend it's not there? As you mark your son's school conference on the calendar, do you wonder how you'll look next to the other parents? Looking at the invitation to your twenty-year high school reunion, do you weigh your successes and failures and look for signs of them in your face and body? If you see only what you want to see, you are about to get a reality check

I want you to stand in front of a full-length mirror and take an objective look at your physical makeup. Use only your eyes. No rose-colored glasses or disgruntled groans. You cannot smile and show only your good side, and you are not permitted to look in the mirror and say, "You disgusting, fat slob." That is not an honest description. That's a social comment.

You've put on twenty pounds in the past year, is a description that tells a truth that you may or may not want to change. You are being truthful so you'll know which features can be taken for granted, which can become selling points, and which may need to be altered or camouflaged. Tell the truth. You're on your own.

Telling the truth is difficult in today's politically correct world.

Several years ago I managed a radio account executive who desperately wanted to get into television sales. She kept me informed of her aspirations and her quest, so I knew each time she applied for a television sales position. Because she was my top biller, I wasn't exactly cheering her on. But after her third unsuccessful try, I called her into my office and asked her if her heart was set on the move into television. She said yes.

"Okay," I said. "Here's what you have to do. You have to lose thirty pounds and buy a more sophisticated wardrobe. After you do those two things, come back to me and I'll give you the buzz words that will clinch the deal in your next interview."

I was her taskmaster, monitoring her progress and getting after her if she faltered.

Six months after our "tell it like it is" conversation, another sales position opened at the television station where she wanted to work. Armed with a new look and a few favorite television management phrases, she won her position.

Technically, she wasn't a better salesperson than she was in her first three interviews. The only thing she did differently in her fourth try was to make a physical impression more compatible with the television industry's standards. The new product she presented was a product they were more apt to buy.

The arrival of computers and entrepreneurs have brought about cultural changes that give sellers more environmental work choices, but this particular seller chose to work in a place where physical appearance was extremely important. She was willing to make personal compromises to get the job she wanted. And lest we leap to judgment about faulty prerequisites, losing thirty pounds was not a bad compromise.

I couldn't give the same advice today, at least in my professional chair. We aren't allowed to make observations that could be deemed prejudicial and therefore tortious, even if asked. In our current politically correct and litigious world, truth all too often takes a back seat to wishful thinking. It's a shame. Denying the truth can delay or even prevent us from reaching our desired results.

We like results, so we're going to tell the truth, even though it may sometimes be unfair or even absurd. You will read stereotypical statements that are discriminatory and disagreeable. But if life is a sales job, and I believe it is, we need to prepare ourselves for life as it is, not as we wish it to be.

Our physical appearance arouses more emotion than any part of our being. It exposes biases and other emotional forces that can be premature and provoke incorrect judgments. People who claim that appearance means nothing to them are intellectually and emotionally bereft or they are ethically unsavory (translated, they lie). It's not possible to avoid forming an opinion regarding the personal appearance of yourself and others. Even creative, free-form individuals form opinions. They may have fewer opinions on this subject than people with more traditional values, but they do have opinions.

Get out pencil and paper and list your physical characteristics, as they exist right now. Attach no value; just write down the facts.

Here is what I look like:

+ Sex

+ Height

+ Weight

+ Ethnic appearance

+ Color: Hair, skin, eyes

+ Distinguishing marks:
  Birthmark, handicaps, teeth, etc.

+ Posture

I purposely left out one physical characteristic. Your voice. While it is physical, it is not immediately apparent upon arrival. The viewer will already have registered a first opinion before you speak. It's a factor we will discuss, but not at first glance.

To illustrate why we're doing this exercise, I'm going to describe the physical characteristics of two people. I guarantee you will make stereotypical judgments as to the rest of their product.

Seller # 1

Male; 6 feet, 5 inches tall; 240 pounds; dark skin, black curly hair; dark brown eyes; powerful stance; African American.

Describe his voice:
Describe his handshake:
Describe his clothing:

Seller # 2

Female; 5 feet, 2 inches tall; 105 pounds; thin, fair skin, straight blond hair; blue eyes; Caucasian, probably northern European; pigeon-toed, head bent slightly forward, chin down.

Describe her voice:
Describe her handshake:
Describe her clothing:

- ◆ Seller # 1 has a deep voice, a firm handshake, and is wearing dark clothing.

- ◆ Seller # 2 has a light, pleasant voice, a wimpy handshake, and is wearing pastel clothing.

Is that what you described? That's what we expect. What if the sellers don't give us what we expect? Will it affect our decision to buy?

A petite blond woman with a husky voice, giving out a firm handshake, wearing a trim black dress will not startle the buyer as much as a large black man with a wispy voice, wimpy handshake, and pastel trousers. The only thing Seller # 2 needs to do to increase her sales power is point her toes forward and lift her head. The man who surprises us has fewer options. An unexpected soft voice in Seller # 1 might actually work to his advantage by reducing the intimidation of his size, but a soft handshake and lavender pants will not work for him in most circles.

A few prejudicial facts:

1. Average size is easier than either small or large for both men and women, although men can get away with a larger extreme than women can. Small is a disadvantage for both sexes.

2. A low, subtle voice register is better for both men and women

than a high, strident pitch. Men can be louder than women can.

3. Direct, steady eye contact is a must, although women can effectively demure at certain moments. Men can't. They appear weak and dishonest.

4. White males have an initial advantage over ethnic minorities and women, in any competitive situation.

5. There is less surprise when minorities and women fail than when white men fail.

6. There is less surprise when white men succeed than when minorities and women succeed. White men are expected to succeed. White men are given more time to succeed because their supervisors feel it reflects on them when white men fail.

7. People are uncomfortable in the presence of illness or physical handicaps, and avoid being in their presence if they can. This is a major disadvantage for people who carry these burdens.

   This is so abhorrent to me that I shudder with fury as I write it, but it's the truth.

8. Posture expresses your confidence level. Sit and stand up straight. Hold your chin in, your shoulders back, and your head up.

9. Women and tall thin men can cross their legs when they sit. Others shouldn't. Women look better if they cross at the ankles. Men should not cross at the ankles. It appears effeminate, and any sign of feminine demeanor in a man is an irritant to most observers. Men can cross their legs only in a casual conversation.

10. Purses are for social situations. Personal items, including money and credit cards, should be kept in a pocket or small container inside a briefcase or professional-looking tote bag. Unless you're in Seattle. Then it's an ugly green Gore-Tex thing.

11. Regionalism is real. Ugly green Gore-Tex marks you as an acceptable native in Seattle. It will mark you as weird in Miami. Get to know and understand the customs of the territory you're in.

Let's test the prejudices.

Today you're a buyer. It's your day off and you need to make two purchases. On your way to buy new underwear, you stop at an auto parts store to purchase a new taillight for your sports utility vehicle.

Who's going to sell you the taillight?

Who's going to sell you the underwear?

If you are male, you will automatically picture a man selling both items. Your second thought will be that you have to place the woman somewhere. She will be selling men's underwear in a department store. Then, thinking this is a trick question to catch the politically incorrect, your third thought will place the woman in both the auto parts store and men's furnishings. This male/female thing still confuses many men.

If you are female, you will put the man in the auto parts store and the woman in lingerie and be done with it. That's the way the world usually works. Some thoughts are easier for women.

Take out your own written physical description. Using what you've learned since you made your objective observations, it's time to apply critical judgment to the facts of your physical appearance.

What do you want to change, and what do you want to keep?

There are prejudices for and against almost everything, so don't change to please someone else. Keep the things you like and the things you cannot change, and modify or remove the rest.

Some modifications will affect reactions more than others will.

If you have brown eyes and you think blue eyes will make you appear more alert, buy blue contact lenses. If you are Asian, it will cause a stir; if you are Caucasian, no one will notice.

If you are fifty pounds overweight, understand that some people will react negatively to your weight, and some professions will be closed to you. If you like the way you look, extra fifty pounds and all, select a field of work where extra weight is not a deterrent.

Fortunately, times are changing, and long-standing prejudices against certain looks for certain jobs are fading. Kathy Bates and John Candy both overcame the notion that you can't play a leading role in a movie unless you weigh under a standard number of pounds in relation to your height. First the movies, then real life.

Do you always have to behave the way you look? Initially, it helps, but always is a long time. Roosevelt Grier, a very large man, wrote a book about needlepoint sewing, which was accepted for publication because he was famous - famous for his feats on the football field. He went with the sure thing for his career, based on his football friendly physical attributes. He retired to do the gentle things he preferred. His nickname is Rosie. That's not exactly the moniker of a giant.

You don't have to wait until retirement to become a more interesting person. You can integrate various styles, regardless of your looks, into your personal and professional lives every day, depending on each day's requirements and goals, and your inclination to stretch your personality.

One successful salesperson I know worked for the radio station that broadcasts the Seattle SuperSonics professional basketball team. His looks were youthful, his stature slight, and his demeanor quiet. At the time, the radio station targeted upscale adults with a news-talk format during the day, and played to sports enthusiasts at night. He dressed in corporate suits for his news-talk presentations, as expected. When he presented the sports packages, he wore green and gold tennis shoes with his suit, which was not expected. Green and gold are, you guessed it, the Sonics' team colors. This small touch changed the atmosphere of the presentation from left-brain ratings statistics to right-brain team emotion. Both presentations were true to the order of the day and neither interfered with Rod's real persona. It worked, of course.

And since we're speaking about appearances, ladies, if you don't want your legs noticed, don't wear miniskirts. If you don't mind comment, either to your face or after you've exited, bless you. Wear whatever you want. I wear miniskirts myself, when I want a personal lift and a change in the atmosphere around me. There's nothing wrong with exposing your better features, as long as you know they will be noticed and noted. It's ridiculous to think otherwise, or to cry foul. On this issue, it's time for women to get real and get over it.

We are judged just by showing up. There's no way around that fact. Our appearance creates an emotional environment for how we behave and how others behave toward us.

To summarize, a large person will initially generate feelings of fear, admiration, intimidation, revulsion, or disrespect, depending on whether large means height or weight. A small person elicits a show-me and prove-yourself response. A handsome person will automatically get the benefit of the doubt. Brains are associated with natural beauty. A homely person faces an uphill battle from the beginning. You have to overcome homely.

People with distinguishing physical characteristics, beneficial or not, at least generate a mindful response. People remember them and they learn to either take advantage of their presence or modify it. They're accustomed to having feedback. Most of us have to discover our physical presence on our own. Look into your mirror carefully. What do you see, and what, if anything, are you going to do about it?

CHAPTER FOUR

The Gut Check

*The product on the inside is your hidden asset. Make sure you
know what's in there and how to use it.*

I COULD PUT TOGETHER a significant list of emotional attributes that would make us better sellers in this job we call life. Most of them would be labeled useful. But there are three character traits that go beyond useful. These three traits, described in depth in this chapter, are critical personal qualities that you will need to access daily in the most visceral sense. Visceral, as in intestinal fortitude, pertaining to instinct rather than intellect.

Your **Gut Check** must reveal these three instincts: **Courage**, **Commitment**, and **Empathy**.

Mr. Webster has two definitions of **Courage**. The first definition says, "The quality of mind or spirit that enables a person to face difficulty, danger, pain, etc., with firmness and without fear."

We are born with courage. We enter this world not in fear, but screaming in rage at this strange, bright, loud, unprotected environment. We don't like this new world and we're not afraid to show it. Eventually our cultural surroundings reduce the level of our rage and we learn to adapt. We are tamed. Some taming is necessary, of course, or we'd eat fur balls and swim into the mouths of snapping crocodiles. To what extent and how we become domesticated determine our ability as adults to meet and overcome challenges. If we are taught to exercise caution in the face of danger, our courage is tractable but undiminished. If our experiences teach us to fear living life to its fullest, our natural courage may be buried. If at least some of our courage remains, we can learn to recall it and use it when we need that extra push of self-esteem to perform at our best when we face difficulties.

We can dispel with part of the definition of courage in our pursuit of selling ourselves by eliminating the fear of facing danger and pain. Nothing you sell, either personally or professionally, should ever subject you to either danger or pain.

That leaves only difficulty…"the quality of mind or spirit that enables a person to face difficulty without fear…."

One of the most effective advertising messages I've ever seen was a full-page magazine ad that said, in bold letters, "**SCARE YOURSELF.** You could be better than you think." The ad triggered a sales meeting in which each of us recalled an instance of fear and shared with the group how we overcame that fear. I've since used this technique in other group situations. The most interesting discovery of this exercise is finding that the most successful people, the individuals who exude the greatest amount of confidence, are the persons who most easily recall fear. As expected, they boldly offer solutions for conquering fear. Yet they are confident enough to admit that they have fears that are hampering their progress. They show no discomfort in putting unresolved fear on the table and asking for help in finding a solution. They are bottom-line problem solvers.

It would appear, then, that courage is not the absence of fear, as the dictionary states. Courage is meeting and overcoming difficulties *in the face of fear*. In fact, further investigation into this subject revealed that the reason successful people can recall moments of fear more quickly than others is because they are constantly pushing themselves into situations that are likely to arouse feelings of fear. They court fear. They enjoy being kept off balance because it hones their ability to push forward. You can't slay dragons if there are no dragons. In light of my findings, I'd like to write another definition of courage.

Courage is the quality of mind and spirit that enables a person to seek and overcome difficulties, even *in the face of fear*.

We want to encourage the spirit of adventure in ourselves, in the people we care for, and in the people we work with. Here are questions to ask as you "seek the spirit" of courage in your life.

1. Have you ever been afraid?

2. Recently?

3. Would you care to describe the situation?

4. How did you get past the fear and solve the problem?

5. Were you pleased with the outcome?

6. Do you welcome opportunities that stretch your levels of comfort?

Fear almost always comes from the unknown. If we can anticipate fear prior to an encounter, we will be more prepared to deal with it and focus on the challenge rather than the fear.

In *advance:*

✦ Anticipate fear.

✦ Knowledge is power. Learn all you can about the challenge.

✦ Make a list of everything you can think of that could go wrong.

✦ Don't manufacture fear. Cut the list.

✦ Write down an item-by-item response to everything still on your list.

✦ If you have no response to some items, set them aside and get more information. You don't have to know everything in advance.

✦ Give yourself time: time to prepare and time to arrive on time.

✦ Have something wonderful to look forward to after the encounter.

The second part of Mr. Webster's definition of Courage is "...to act in accordance with one's beliefs, especially in spite of criticism."

The second part is vital. If you are in a healthy environment, you should feel free to offer your personal style, ideas, and opinions, even though they may differ from the existing culture, without fear of repercussions. People should be allowed to exist in a community where there are differences. Healthy relationships and companies welcome diverse appearances and ideas. If the environment is sound, your courage may have to cover disappointment when you learn that, even in a healthy setting where your personal style is welcome and you are treated as an equal, not all your ideas and opinions will become courses of action. Courage also means the ability to accept the fact that yours is not the only voice of reason.

Unfortunately, some environments are not emotionally healthy enough to accept a variety of styles and opinions. If you decide the overall benefits of staying in a place on the short side of Shangri-La outweigh the handicaps, you need courage to continue to offer input and accept critical response as part of the price you pay for exercising your freedom of expression. And if the level of criticism is more than you are prepared to tolerate, you may have to summon the courage to leave, either through your choice or the disposition of the offended parties.

In any environment, if your input is not being well received, examine possible reasons for the rejection. Solicit the assistance of a friendly face. There may be valid reasons why your ideas are not being implemented. It could be a matter of timing, or polishing a few delivery points, or addressing the objections of one or two persons. These are surface problems that can be overcome. If it is a difference in basic beliefs, however, seek a more suitable environment. The battle of basic beliefs cannot be won.

Which brings us to **Commitment.** It's not fair to yourself, or your clients or partners, to leave any one of you waiting in the wings after Act 1, anticipating Acts 2 and 3, if you don't have the courage to commit yourself to performing them.

"Commitment denial" is the label applied to the flower flakes of the sixties. During the decade of glorious self-discovery, all we wanted was freedom from financial shackles to discover our inner souls. We willingly gave up the single-minded pursuit of material goods for more idealistic causes. Well, as the song goes, "Freedom's just another word for nothing left to lose...." We decided some things weren't worth losing, so we went back to work and began gathering goods again, but with less fervor than before. We were willing to strike a balance between ideals and possessions. The "commitment denial" label no longer fits.

The upside of our freedom to ride on both sides of the track is the satisfaction of knowing we questioned, selected, and earned our lifestyle. Our parents gave us material goods and we opted to give back their belongings and fight for our own ideals. We may have ended our quest for freedom right back in the middle of the road, but we got there not by entitlement, but by commitment. The downside of our revolution is that our children have been given both freedom and material goods without a struggle. They have nothing to rebel against and nothing to fight for. There is no revolution on their horizon and apparently no inclination to find or develop one. What do they have to commit to? Their long-term employment is a major trial facing the business world today. The challenge is to find a fire that will burn in their bellies long enough to entice commitment.

First, let's establish that individual freedom, though it has brought us new challenges in the pursuit of greater discovery, is a GOOD thing. The major responsibilities of society's physical, emotional, and financial growth will always lie with the individual's commitment to greatness. There is much left for new generations to conquer. We should encourage our children to challenge us, even though their awakening may bring us discomfort. Freedom requires a renewed commitment from each generation.

What's good about freedom today?

1. Equal opportunity has given us a broader spectrum of people to share the workload. The increase in actual participants gives us more ideas and hands with which to expand our goals.

2. Achieving life balance is accepted and expected. Taking home a paycheck is not the only standard for measuring satisfaction. We are freer to pursue personal interests.

3. We have more career options. Very few people stay with one job for a lifetime. Career mobility is a reality.

4. Living as a single person is an acceptable lifestyle. People who opt against marriage and family are no longer social outcasts.

5. Our choices in every aspect of our lives are far greater than they were before the decade of self-discovery.

What's the downside?

1. We have to **commit** to encouraging the diversity of participants.

2. We have to **commit** to expanding our personal interests.

3. We have to **commit** to exploring career options to keep our workplace knowledge current.

4. We may have to **commit** to something or someone—company

or companion—to fully realize and enjoy our freedom, even though living singly is accepted.

5. We have to **commit** to the revival of dreams. They used to come naturally.

The difference between a starving artist who is remembered and a starving artist who is forgotten is **commitment.** The difference between dreams living and dreams dying is **commitment**. Do you have dreams worthy of your **commitment**? Have I highlighted the word **commitment** enough? It's the future and it's important.

Empathy is the ability to identify with the feelings, thoughts, and attitudes of another person. Without empathy, you will have no idea what kind of approach you will need to take to trigger another person's decision to buy. Without knowing what he or she is thinking and feeling you will not be able to sell an idea. You may be able to get a signed contract, but without a commitment to the idea behind it, it will become the contract from hell. If the customer is not sold on the idea, he will find a way to get out of it or make you wish you had never brought him into it. Without empathy, you won't know why this wonderful deal went south, or why this crummy person is making your life miserable. You will hate him and not know why, and there is no satisfaction in hating someone unless you know why.

Seriously folks, there is no substitute for empathy. It is the one trait that cannot be taught. You either have it, or you don't. Since I am a lifetime problem solver, this bothers me. I have spent many frustrating hours trying to teach empathetically vacuous people how to sell. Whenever we enter a discussion that focuses on the buyers' needs or the reasons why we must listen carefully, they tune out. They simply see no need to spend what they consider to be wasted time on another point of view.

If you are in a position of hiring personnel, there are two components of a sale that may expose the absence of empathy in a salesperson. The trick is to be able to examine these elements prior to offering a position to a person who lacks this key trait.

1. The *closing ratio* is very telling. If a person initiates a lot of calls, gets a lot of appointments, and makes a lot of presentations, but gets very few orders from his activities, this person is not connecting on a gut level with his potential customers.

   Sales being a numbers game, the seller may be making enough calls to reap enough sales to bring in enough revenues to make budget. In fact, people with low empathy make more cold calls than other sellers do. They learn that they have to make more calls to keep their numbers up.

   If they are willing to make the calls and in fact are producing revenues, why wouldn't you want these people on your sales staff regardless of their empathy quotient?

2. *Poor customer service,* or no customer service at all, will bring customer complaints. Salespersons lacking in empathy could cost you as much business as they bring in. Their interest lies only in the planting, not in the irrigation or harvesting for another season. You can't afford to lose this year's customers when next year's sales projections are handed down.

How do you uncover an empathy void prior to hiring? It's difficult, but there are certain questions to ask that will give you a better chance for discovery.

1. Ask an applicant to tell you the three most important questions to ask a client.

2. Ask him if he has questions for you. See if he asks you the same three questions. Then ask if he has any more questions. He should have at least one more question to separate his interest in you from his interest in the rest of the pack. Empathy is about getting personal.

3. Ask him to give examples of how he has helped other people get something they wanted.

4. Ask him to describe the last time he *gave* something away.

I know people who do not have the capacity to empathize. Some of them have made a great deal of money. They force their wares and ideas onto other people. If money is your only barometer of success, you may say that empathy is not a necessary trait for achieving everything you want. And you would be correct, given your limited criteria. But most of the successes enjoyed by people without empathy are temporary, and most of these people end up alone and wondering why.

People find ways to get out of forced deals. People gravitate toward those who care, and leave those who don't. Money fills many voids, and I'd rather have more of it than less, but not at the expense of long-term relationships. Selling is a cooperative effort, and I wouldn't want it any other way.

We've covered what I believe are the Big Three in Gut Checks: **Courage**, **Commitment**, and **Empathy**. There are numerous other personal attributes that are helpful. I encourage you to find your most useful gut checks to keep you on track toward reaching your goals. Here are a few of my personal favorites.

Humor: I couldn't get along without it. I almost made humor a mandatory trait because it is so useful for reducing tension and keeping a perspective. But I know enough good, successful people who don't have it, so I left it off the list. These people don't have as much fun as I do, but they manage to get along just fine.

Focus: A necessary skill, but not necessarily a trait. Focus can be systemically taught. The trick is to find the right system. Unless a system can be used quickly and without thought, it is a focus distraction rather than an improvement.

Competition: You will have to score wins to stay on the winning track. Winning over your competition means beating them. They don't have to lose, but you want them to finish behind you. If you have trouble with this, you may not be suited to sales as a career. Winning over your clients and loved ones is wooing them. This is a pleasure. It's a win/win situation. Winning over your own achievements is growth. This is satisfaction. It is invigorating. If you need to develop a winning attitude, you can cultivate a more competitive disposition by keeping company with winners or enrolling in aggressiveness training courses.

Communication: Absolutely necessary, but again, a skill that can be learned with specific training. Even natural communicators need help in developing new skills to work with additional responsibilities and expanding technology. Because we must work more efficiently to keep pace with technological advances, there is an increased need for better telephone interaction techniques and more concise writing skills. Bullet points have replaced paragraphs. In addition, we all must learn to be proficient in the use of on-line technology. Even though face-to-face communication is still the most effective setting for the completion of personal and business transactions, the arrival of commonly used technological advances has reduced the amount of time we have for finishing our projects. Communication skills in our changing times have to be consistently reviewed, renewed, and updated.

Health: Take care of yourself. Be as healthy as you can be. Feel as good as you can, make your thoughts as positive as you can, and look as good as you can. For personal reasons, health would be at the top of my list of necessary ingredients for leading a successful life. Both my parents died young. I miss them and I'm angry with them for not taking better care of their health.

Also for personal reasons, I have to temper my emphasis on physical health as a necessary trait. Former Congresswoman Barbara Jordan and preeminent cosmologist Stephen Hawking are my most influential heroes. Both of them managed to contribute a great deal toward the betterment of our world in spite of having to live with physical frailty. They've helped me to understand that we must accept the fact that our bodies may present us with limitations that are beyond our control. I've become more tolerant in my feelings about boundaries.

My heroes also prove emphatically that first impressions can be overcome. After you get to know your mirror image, take a long look inside the shell you see and discover the important assets you carry inside. You have to consciously work at revealing them and using them to your advantage.

CHAPTER FIVE

Prepare Yourself to Be Lucky

*Luck comes to everyone. Only a few people recognize it.
Fewer still are prepared to do something about it.*

I WISH I COULD TAKE CREDIT for the title of this chapter, "Prepare Yourself To Be Lucky," but it was the title of a speech that the late former Secretary of State Dean Rusk gave in an address while he was tenured at the University of Georgia. It speaks to the luck that successful people seem to have.

We're responsible for most of what happens to us, but not all of it. The events that happen to us, rather than the events we make happen, are called luck. Do you believe in luck?

When I posed that question to people I knew, the answer, without exception, was yes. In fact, all of them said they'd personally experienced the anomaly of luck. They said, with more than a little tongue in cheek, that bad luck happens to them and good luck happens to everyone else.

Nice try. Although it's tough to admit, most of our misfortunes are the result of faulty judgment, careless action, and the absence of a cohesive plan. If we are going to get past our problems and prevent their recurrence, we have to accept responsibility for our errors and recognize bad luck for what it is.

We are not responsible for the stray bullet that crashes through the front window of our home. It is a frightening and dangerous case of bad luck. Nothing we could have done would have prepared us for this instant of terror. There was no advance notice and no way of knowing this would happen. Our responsibility lies in how we handle the result of this kind of bad luck. We can let it take over our life, or we can actively do something to get past it. We can ask for spiritual or professional guidance for ourselves, and we can join with the community to take specific action to stop senseless violence.

The stray bullet was bad luck for the homeowner. However, it was not bad luck for the person holding the gun. The fact that the bullet strayed was a product of careless action in the handling of the gun. The fact it was shot at all was an act of faulty judgment. The person who shot the gun is wholly responsible for what happened, and should be held solely accountable.

I've purposely used an extreme example to prove an important point. Aside from how and to whom it happens, the main difference between bad luck and good luck is the lack of control we have over bad luck and the influence we can have over the arrival of good luck. We can *prepare* ourselves to be lucky.

Synonyms for the word **lucky** are successful, prosperous, thriving, flourishing, gaining, winning, overcoming. Action words. Lucky people don't wait around. They actively seek their fortunes.

Where do we start? Well... Uh... I don't know. Where are we going? That's a problem and it's a common one. If we don't know where we're going, we don't know how to start or where to go. We're standing here, feet glued to the floor, rear end stuck to the chair, because until now we didn't know where to begin.

We are going to begin by coming up with a name for our fortune and we will call it a **GOAL.** We're going to achieve our goal by moving ahead to the finish line and working our way back to the starting gate. What does the finish line look like?

A Goal Must Have
Certain Identifiable Characteristics

A goal must be:

PERSONAL   You have to have a stake in the outcome.

PASSIONATE   You have to really, really want it.

WRITTEN   There must be hard-copy proof that you have a
                goal.

SPECIFIC   State exactly what the goal is in one simple sen-
                tence or phrase. "I'd like to be happy" is not a
                goal. It's an emotion. It may come as a result of
                achieving a goal. "I'd like to have $10,000 in my
                savings account by the end of this year" is a goal.
                Reaching it may make you happy.

ACHIEVABLE   There may be physical, legal, or technical rea-
                sons why a goal is not possible to attain in your
                lifetime. Riding a rocket ship to the stars is not
                possible until the technology exists to get you
                there. If you are 5'2" and female, you probably
                won't play in the NBA no matter how much you
                love to shoot baskets. Don't waste your time pin-
                ing for what you cannot achieve.
                    On the other hand, don't limit yourself unnec-
                essarily. You can achieve more than you think.
                Tom Wittaker lost a foot and part of a leg in an
                automobile accident in 1979 and stood on top of
                Mt. Everest in 1998, an ascent of seemingly
                impossible odds.

COMPATIBLE   Don't fight yourself. There may be cultural, emo-
                tional, or social reasons why a specific goal is not

appropriate for you. If you have a loathsome fear of snakes, don't volunteer for Peace Corps duty in the Amazon. If you are an animal rights protectionist, don't go to the opera. (I'm sorry. Forget I said that. It just slipped out - not my fault. Bad luck.)

TIMEBOUND   Determine a specific amount of time to reach the finish line. It could be five hours or five years, but in order to effectively evaluate the worthiness of your pursuit and keep yourself on the straight and efficient path, you need to know how long it will take to pocket your fortune.

INCREMENTAL   The lunar "Giant Step for Mankind" began with baby steps on earth. A miler sets quarter-mile checkpoints to make sure the pacing along the way will keep the finish line time bound. Incremental steps also create reward opportunities along the way to keep motivation at a goal-achievement level.

REPLACEABLE   If a goal turns out to be unworthy or ill timed, ditch it. Be careful you don't use this escape hatch as an excuse to flake out. If you decide you need to shelve a goal, insert a new goal immediately.

When one goal is nearly complete, write down your next goal. **This is very important**. It's not unusual to have an emotional letdown following the rush of success.

These are not new rules. They've been handed out in some form at nearly every motivational seminar I've attended over the years. They are worth restating, but rules alone will not get you to the starting gate. You still need the action plan. It's printed here for you to copy and use. Get out your pen and paper—or your computer—and prepare yourself to be lucky.

What do you want to accomplish in the foreseeable future?

Write down three goals.

1. _____

2. _____

3. _____

Select the one goal that is most important to you right now.

Is it personal? Is it desirable? Is it specific, achievable, compatible, time bound, measurable, and replaceable?

Write it down

_____

_____

_____

You have established your most desirable goal and you've written it down. We've got the finish line. Now we go to the starting gate and begin our push forward.

The physical roadblocks to achievement of my goal are:
(Personal handicaps, technology, geographic location, financial)

1. _____

2. _____

3. _____

4. _____

The steps I must take to get past these roadblocks are:

There could be several steps for each roadblock. List them separately on another piece of paper.

The cultural, emotional, and social roadblocks that are not compatible are:

1. _____

2. _____

3. _____

4. _____

The steps I must take to get past these roadblocks are:

There could be several steps for each roadblock. List them separately on another piece of paper.

Establish a time table:

Dates of Checkpoints: 1. _____

                          2. _____

                          3. _____

Date of finish line: 4. _____

Proof of results: *(one for each date)*

1. _____

2. _____

3. _____

4 _____

These are my rewards: *(one for each checkpoint)*

1. _____

2. _____

3. _____

4. _____

Mission Accomplished.

_____   _____
(Your signature)   (Second signature)

Your signature is a binding commitment to yourself to get to the finish line.

The second signature is reserved for a special person who will commit to supporting your goal and stay with you from the starting gate to the finish line. Choose someone who cares enough to give you some flack if you waiver. This person will deserve a BIG reward when you reach your goal.

You were initially asked to write down three goals, and select your favorite as your primary project. That doesn't mean the other two should be ignored or discarded. They were important enough to write down. Follow through on them. They can be your next goals that begin when goal number one is complete, or you may choose to work on one of them concurrently with your first goal.

There is no reason why you can't work on more than one goal at a time, provided they are not conflicting, and together do not take too much of your time and energy. One goal could be personal and one professional. You can allocate different time segments, different energy sources, and different co-signers to work on each of them.

Whether you work on one or more than one goal, you will need to have your replacement goals ready when your first goals are nearly realized. Write them down now. You want your good luck to continue.

CHAPTER SIX

The Computers Have Landed

The most significant change in product production since the dawning of the industrial age has revolutionized the way products are positioned and sold. The Computer Age has arrived.

THE COMPUTERS HAVE LANDED and they are carrying alien forces. Computers themselves obviously have changed our way of doing business, but the people who created and developed computers for our homes, offices, and the community at large have changed the way we conduct business and manage our personal lives far more than the products they have produced. The leaders of the Computer Age are not the same kind of people who led us through the Industrial Age.

Industrialists were manual artists with traditional work habits and lifestyle goals. Their focus was on production levels rather than product innovation. They were more interested in building cars that looked better by their standards than in creating cars that ran better by consumer, environmental, and cost efficiency standards. Foreign competition forced design changes in American cars, and U.S. government regulations, put into action by consumer advocacy groups, forced better fuel efficiency. Early industrialists had the economic power to ignore the marketplace. They believed their preferences reflected marketplace standards. They gave their customers what they believed they should have, based on what they liked themselves. They played the role of the good, wise parent who dishes out vitamins inserted in great globs of peanut butter to the children.

I've used the automobile industry as an example, but by the early 1980's, the distribution of a wide variety of foreign products began to eat into American product sales. The rest of the world was manufacturing smaller, more efficient, technologically superior products and delivering them to American consumers. The United States' industrial superiority was being seriously challenged on the consumer front line. It was 1957 and Sputnik all over again. But not to fear. America regained the Space Age advantage and would recapture the dollars of the American consumer as well. Temporary complacency caused a little setback, but it was nothing permanent, and no cause to change corporate cultures.

Then along came the Computer Age to chip (forgive me) away at the gross national sales percentages formerly held by industrialists. Computer products are not competitive products, they are new products. And their creators are not the same good old boys. They definitely have their own clubhouse rules.

Industrialists like to see tangible signs of progress and success. Obsolete is the tail fin. If I continue to drive a perfectly serviceable car with tail fins, when rounded rear ends are the most recent production change, I'm not on the winning team. To win I need to buy their new cars and do my banking with the big city block guys. Industrialists are uncomfortable if they don't get haircuts every two weeks and wear dark colored suits.

Computer people tinker with their minds. Microsoft managers "re-org" their programming groups periodically, moving people to different departments, not because they aren't doing well where they are, but because they want them to learn to do well in *other* departments to keep their minds alert and interdepartmental competition flowing.

Computer innovation focuses on changing the product from the inside out. The computer I bought this year looks the same as the computer my daughter bought a few years ago. Mine computes faster and holds more information than hers, but you couldn't tell that by looking at it. The cars that computer developers drive can be ten-year-old pickups or brand new Mercedes four-door sedans. A Mercedes owner's friends and colleagues can drive ten-year-old pickups if they want to, and park them right next to her new Mercedes. It doesn't matter. Money and prestige are not issues. A used pickup that runs well is as good as a new Mercedes, if that's what the owner wants to drive.

The progression of how computers were initially sold as an extension of business systems to governments and large manufacturers, to how personal computers are sold today as a standalone entity to schools, homes, and small businesses, is a fascinating study in the evolution of how products are put in the hands of consumers and merits discussion here.

International Business Machines (IBM) is the most notable company to enter into and initially succeed in the development and sale of computers. It was considered the hallmark of product innovation in an industrial environment. IBM defined its computer products and computer customers in the same traditional vein as its mainline business machine products and customers.

IBM's business machines were designed and manufactured to be marketed to CEOs of very successful, well established companies, whose corporate cultures were cautious and conservative. It saw nothing new, sexy, or exciting about the arrival of computers. They were merely an extension of its current product line. It saw nothing new, sexy, or exciting about the potential buyers. They were the same old customers buying a new form of the same old product. There was nothing new, sexy, or exciting about the way computers should be sold. Same sellers, same positioning.

They were called "The Men in Blue." Describe one, describe them all. Caucasian men with Ivy League degrees, close-cropped hair, and dark blue suits, just like their owners and managers. They carried snap-shut briefcases holding order forms ready for the gathering of guaranteed signatures.

Everyone recognized that, over time, computers would become the standard mode of worldwide systems and operations. Eventually there would be a complete shift away from the clickety clack of basic mechanical operations to the quiet downloading of complex analytical systems. IBM and its customers were methodically preparing for the technical changes in the products they would be selling and using. There was no need to push the envelopes faster. What worked for business machines would work for computers. IBM would sell its computers to the same organizations to whom it sold its business machines. Nothing would change. IBM owned the market and it would control the market.

Isn't hindsight amazing? IBM and its customers assumed they would own the market forever. They assumed a status quo, even though the history of our known world has proved there is no such thing. Expand or contract is the ruling law of the universe. Even after the United States government decided to cut IBM down to a more manageable size, it was too big to be out done. IBM threw more bucks at lobbyists and made the government go away —*for thirteen years!*

But IBM's time-tested strategies failed to take into account how soon and how much the arrival of computers would change the world's economic and social structures. It was lulled into the complacency of its own time lines and the limitations of its historically narrow horizons. It failed to pay attention to the prowess and the pacing of the boys from Microsoft. Bill Gates and his cohorts were well regarded as computer people with valuable technical knowledge, but disregarded as a serious business threat. Microsoft virtually stole the software industry out from under IBM, and accelerated the transformation from the Industrial Age to the Computer Age, by quickly developing its own product and encouraging the entry of new computer companies eager to climb aboard its fast track to the future.

1. The development of computers brought about a complete change in productive thought processes and the profiles of the people who affected the change. Talented mainstream mechanical engineers gave way to talented introspective mathematicians.

2. The use of computers required more complex operational skills from the highest to the lowest levels of production and management. You can no longer start your engines, gentlemen, with the push of a single button. You have to understand how the components of the engines work in order to push the right buttons. You have to **think** before you **push**. *Everyone* has to learn or relearn how to do the simplest business tasks. This has equalized performance levels. Caste separations are becoming blurred. Who's in charge here?

3. Some jobs become obsolete. New jobs have to be created. Many bright, experienced people in the work force either have to be retrained or replaced. This is not a new phenomenon. Every generation must deal with the professional displacement of a segment of the population. What is new this time is the accompanying prevalent change from **rote** to **innovation**.

   Manual laborers will not find new jobs. Clerical workers become middle managers. The emerging new middle class is in the infrastructure of the workplace. Computers have eliminated certain low-paying jobs and created fewer, but higher paying, positions. The laws of supply and demand have given the techies the hiring edge. The cost of payroll has not gone down.

   Company owners may have to cover the growing middle class by reducing the upper class. Uh-oh, more innovators displacing traditionalists. Alien clout is rising.

4. Innovators, by definition, are not as concerned with tradition. Social acceptance is not high on the list of needs for these computer folks. They figure they can get just as much done in a pair of jeans as they can in a suit and tie. Revise that. They think they can get *more* done in jeans. They wear jeans to work. Casual Friday is a by-product of the techies' everyday routine. They also think they can get more done in the quiet of the computer room at home than in the bustle of workplace coffee klatches and ringing telephones. Company employees don't

want to work at work. It's no longer how ya' gonna keep 'em down on the farm, but how ya' gonna keep 'em off the farm and in the office.

Which brings us to...

5. The single, most important shift in the computer world is the role of the entrepreneur. With a computer in my home I can be a competitive force with almost anyone. While we don't know how long individual entrepreneurs will stay in business, we do know that in a very short period of time Amazon.com sold millions of books to hundreds of thousands of customers who did not walk into bookstores to make their purchases.

   Don't look now, but employees may become their employer's toughest competitors. Home offices don't have to carry the overhead of high rises. Customers don't care how much it costs you to run a business. They care about how much it costs them to buy your product. How do you build customer loyalty these days? How do you build employee loyalty?

You build loyalty by making the benefits of working with you outweigh the benefits of working without you. But you have to know what is meant by benefits. Is it time? Money? Security? Atmosphere? What's a traditional manager to do? Computer aliens have messed up our tidy world. Here's an example of what happens:

1. IBM and its customers had to consider these upstarts and their computers to be worthy competitors.

2. In order to compete, IBM and its customers had to bring a few of these innovators to work for them.

3. In order to compete, IBM had to expand its customer base to include new, smaller companies. This posed more questions -

does it spend less time with long standing customers, or does it increase its work force to cover the new customers?

4. In order to compete, IBM customers had to consider proposals from companies other than IBM, to make sure they were receiving the latest technology and information at the most beneficial pricing. Price may not have been an issue between old, trusted business partners.

5. Both IBM and its customers had to adjust their corporate cultures to attract and keep the new innovators, without going so far as to lose the traditionalists that still constitute most of the bread and butter accounts that bring in the bottom line.

6. Both IBM and its customers had to expand their sales and promotional strategies to attract new customers and tickle the fancies of the new economically powerful creative people who, up until now, have shown more than a little ambivalence towards traditional sales pitches.

IBM and its long-term customers have made these changes and are finding new ways to compete effectively in the new worlds of computer company cultures and home offices. And please understand, IBM and its old-line customers are not the only companies that found themselves operating in a world completely different from their worlds of only a decade ago. They are merely examples of a world of change.

Now the United States government, with suggestive money coming from Microsoft's competitors, feels the need to cut Microsoft down to size. Microsoft thought it could be successful indefinitely without greasing the palms of politicians. Its products were so good and so consumer based, it thought it couldn't possibly be challenged by the people elected to protect consumers and free market trade. Like all that have gone before, Microsoft misjudged the level of the competition. The conservative thinkers are not going to relinquish their power without a heck of a fight, and they shouldn't. Worthy competition begets progress.

Microsoft is now beginning to pay the price of its own version of status quo, which is, what it thinks is important is equally important to everyone else. The company began to whistle its own version of daddy knows all. Nuts and bolts still hold much of our society together and traditional thinking still has enormous buying power. Microsoft is now the number one technical company in terms of political donations, and Mr. Gates is almost always photographed in a suit these days.

There are no more creative thinkers today than there were a decade ago, nor are there fewer traditionalists. The difference is not in numbers of people whose inclinations lie on either side of the thought processes. The difference is in the stature and economic power of the creative mind. Determining how to trigger buying decisions in this new era of conservative and innovative equality is a far more complex and challenging process than it was when the power lay decidedly with the more solid, sensible, and predictable left side of the brain.

Is this good news for sellers, or what?!?

I believe that IBM and Microsoft once were technical equals, and perhaps they still are. But Microsoft has won the sales war.

IBM kept its product development teams in the back rooms. The men in blue continued to be its only sign of life to the outside world. Its front team continued to sell their *Personal* Computers in the corporate image. Would I buy my first home computer from the men in blue? Possibly. But the bigger question is, would they even think to ask me? Who are they selling their Personal Computers to? Not to *this* person.

Bill Gates, product innovator, number one techie, back-room brain-stormer, company owner, is also Number One Seller. *He sold his personal product his way*, to anyone who would listen to his story. He made computer products seem personal.

I'm not buying some nameless Microsoft product. I'm buying Bill's software. He asked *me* to buy his very own personal product. I've never met the man, but I know Mr. Gates. Not only does he own and operate the largest computer software company in the world, he sings "Twinkle Twinkle Little Star" to his little girl. He said so on Barbara Walters' program on television. Before you cynics throw up, think about what he's done. His television commercials say, "Where in the **World** do *you* want to go today?" His television interview says, "I'm just like you. I'm your next door **Neighbor**." He's not Bill Gates, President of Microsoft worldwide. He's Mr. Rogers, and he's in my neighborhood!

Is the successful sale of Microsoft products to the world and me just the luck of an enthusiastic product developer, or the result of a very shrewd, long-term strategy? I think Bill Gates knew what he was doing every step of the way. He prepared himself to be lucky, and he has forever changed the way successful marketers sell their products. He's made the world a smaller market. He sells the same brand of products to homemakers in Fargo, North Dakota, and corporate executives in London, England. *Personal* computer products? Get outta here! There is absolutely *nothing* personal about computer products.

What's personal is the enthusiastic and creative selling of a product by a person who passionately believes in the product. The product is himself.

Very few people have the selling acumen of Bill Gates, with the ability to reach both housewives and corporate executives. If that were the case, we'd see a shift of emphasis from the blustering personality to a thoughtful and caring temperament in the hiring of salespeople. That's not happening, and it shouldn't. We're not looking for a shift from one sales type to another. Hopefully we've learned the folly of a singular approach, and we will expand our perceptions of what it takes to be an effective seller, rather than rush to embrace the sales technique of the day. Traditional judgment as to what it takes to sell the world's products will have to bow to the building of sales teams with enough individuality and versatility to service the increasing assortment of customers and suppliers now making buying decisions.

If people are allowed to use their individual assets to the fullest, they are more likely to work with confidence and sell more product. The cultural changes that have come about as a result of the acceptance of individual taste make it more important than ever for sellers to carefully examine the components of what their personal product has to offer to the customer. The person who is selling is more important than the product that is being sold. That has always been the case. Thanks to the arrival of the Computer Age, what good sellers have always known has been validated.

Opportunities are increasing for different kinds of personalities to succeed in sales. Sales is a great gig, and I welcome the new company and the increased competition.

CHAPTER SEVEN

What Sales Isn't

Sales is not a dishonorable or sleazy way
to steal from unsuspecting innocents.

IN SPITE OF THE FACT that there have been meaningful changes in how products are marketed to the public, there still are people who are afraid of being sold. They give sellers a bad rap, so we'll identify them and make sure we're ready to deal with them.

"Who sold you that car, Harry?" "Nobody. Bought it myself." Harry's afraid to admit that a seller may have influenced his decision to make a purchase. Falling under the influence of a disreputable salesperson is such a prevalent fear that the word "sales" seldom appears on the business card of a sales representative. We're labeled "Marketing Representatives" or "Account Executives" or whatever happens to be the cover-up term of the day. Yessir. Harry bought it himself. Not a salesperson around.

I believe this unfounded aversion to sellers comes from three sources, the same three sources that generate most of our prejudicial feelings: **Insecurity**, **Ignorance**, and **Bad Apples**.

Let's talk about **Bad Apples** first. They are the simplest sources of prejudice to explain, because they are tangible beings and are easy to identify. Here are three buying scenarios. One of them has a bad apple.

1. You go to the market to buy a bag of apples. Gravensteins are in season and the price at this market is reasonable and competitive with other markets. If the product is good, this is where you'll buy your apples. You pick up each apple and personally inspect it. You make your selection based on each apple's individual color and firmness. You take your selection to the cashier and make your purchase. No bad apples in this bunch.

2. You're out for a Sunday drive. You see a roadside fruit stand. The sign says "100 Boxed Apples for $10." Not Gravenstein, not personally inspected, but only $10. ONLY $10! You buy a whole box of apples for about the same price as the small bag of apples you purchased the previous Sunday at the market. You take them home and sort them out. There are ten mushy apples and two more that are actually turning brown. But there were no claims of perfection, and nearly 90% of the apples are good. The price gave you a clue that they would not have the same quality as the apples you hand-picked at a higher price. It was still a good buy and you'd go back there again. There are only a few bad apples.

3. The following Sunday, another drive, another apple stand with the same message: "100 Apples for $10." You buy yourself another hundred apples. (You obviously have an apple fetish.) Underneath the top layer of red, crisp bargain apples are four layers of mushy, nearly rotten apples. *You've been had.* There are twenty good apples and eighty bad apples - 80% of the apples are bad. But forget about the apple numbers. The apples in the box are not to blame. There really is only one bad apple, and that is the person who sold you this miserable box of apples.

You have several options as to what to do about your experience with the BIG BAD APPLE:

a) Give up all apples. One bad apple spoils them all.

b) Give up all roadside stand apples. One bad apple spoils them all.

c) Go back to the second apple stand and pelt the S.O.B. with the rotten apples he sold you. Take out the Big Bad Apple.

d) Dig a little deeper into the roadside boxes before you buy. Some boxes are better than others.

e) Dig a little deeper into who's selling the apples. Since the market apples were good and the first roadside apples were pretty good, not all apple sales are bad. *One bad apple seller doesn't spoil all apple sales.*

Eliminate option c). He's not worth the trouble you'll get into for your brief moment of satisfaction.

The choice here is option e). Behind every one of your apple purchases there was a seller. You were not choosing the apples; you were choosing the sellers of the apples. You experienced two good apple sellers and one bad apple seller. Don't give up on all apple sellers because of one bad apple seller. If you learn to pick the sellers with the same care you use when you pick their products, you will eliminate the bad apple source of sales prejudice.

Insecurity is not so easily eliminated. People spend millions of dollars in psychiatrists' offices each year trying to find the root of their insecurities so they can overcome them and move forward. We're not going there. We're going to consider only two simple aspects of insecurity stemming from society's demand for competition. It's the "I'm-better-than-you-are, therefore I-should-win-and-you-should-lose" system.

The first aspect makes me nuts. It's **Elitism**. It's snobbery. It's meaningless competition. It's insecurity, and it keeps us from recognizing and applauding the vast majority of people who make our societies work. We all want to be contributors to a well-run community and feel that we offer something of value to the world we live in. The problem with elitism is that a few people have gained power through education, money, and/or cronyism, and they feel that what they accomplish is more important than what the less educated, less affluent, social no-names achieve by merely tackling the dailies. Elitism is hogwash and it riles me faster than anything else I can think of.

I am a seller, personally and professionally. Over the years, my personal handle has remained the same. My name is Shirley Thom and what you see is what you get, always. My professional names have changed, however, and with each new change in labeling, I've been able to access different doors.

1. Shirley Thom, Salesperson, NE: Account Executive, gets to meet with the Advertising Agency's Media Buyer, who by the way, controls most of the expenditures of the client's money even though his or her position is one of advertising's bottom rungs in esteem and take-home pay. Media Buyers are too close to the sales process to be paid the big bucks.

2. Shirley Thom, Sales Manager, gets to meet with the Media Supervisor in the agency, and sometimes even the Account Supervisor, who has direct access to THE CLIENT. As sales manager I can't quite open the door yet to the office of THE CLIENT. Even though the addition of the word "Manager" has elevated my access to certain people, the word "sales" is still there, and THE CLIENT must be protected from that disgusting sales thing.

3. Shirley Thom resigned from her sales manager position and started her own company, and put the word "President" on her business card. One person, with no source of income, working out of her house, became president of her own company. She could pick up the phone, connect with the office of THE CLIENT, identify herself as a president, and ask to speak to THE CLIENT. "Yes, Ms. Thom, I'll put you through." The last door is open to the President.

It's easy to play the Elitism game. By calling myself "President," I gained access. In a social setting, I say I own my own company and accept looks of approval from the same people whose eyes glazed over six months earlier when I only sold advertising. Like the people I disdain, I play the game. It still makes me nuts.

In my version of a perfect world the garbage collector would attend the same party as the corporate executive, and when I ask him what kind of work he does, he would hand me a business card that says "Garbage Collector" rather than "Sanitary Engineer." Then I'd know exactly what he does and I could thank him for performing a magnificent service. But this is not a perfect world, so we must accept the existence of elitism.

But we needn't be cowed by it. On days you feel particularly put upon as a seller, pretend your business cards say "President" and launch into sales negotiations as if you own the joint. Oh why pretend? Go out and buy yourself 50 business cards that say you are a president. It's easily done. Carry them with you the next time you go some place where you expect to meet pretentious idiots. Hand out your president cards and see what happens. Power, even pseudo power, is a wonderful security enhancement.

The second source of sales insecurity is what I call the **Small Patatah**. You're just a little spud sittin' in the dirt waiting to be exposed. The only way you feel you're as big as anyone else is to avoid those you think are bigger. You refuse to be sold. You pretend that sellers don't exist, or if they do, they're to be avoided.

The difference between Elitism and Small Patatah has to do with the source of the insecurity. Elitism is the other guy trying to control you by comparing himself favorably over you. He believes he is bigger, brighter, and better looking than you are, and therefore, you don't belong in the same room. He doesn't think you can compete.

Small Patatah is yourself believing the crap the other guy is dishing out. Let's figure out why you believe it and what you can do to believe in yourself rather than self-serving elitist oafs. Bottom line is, that's why I am writing this book. I'd like to see more people enter the open fields of work and play, and have the tools to effectively compete.

Competing in an arena of equality is an exhilarating and positive adventure. Whether we believe in Divinity or Darwin, or both, we've always existed in a world of competition. We always will. It's inherent in our nature and it's how we grow. That's why I dislike elitism so adamantly. It's a rite of exclusion that stifles growth.

The antithesis of growth is **Ignorance**, the last of our proposed sources of sales prejudice. Taken within this small frame of reference, ignorance can be overcome. Knowledge derails ignorance. Knowledge of our allies, our obstacles, and ourselves moves us past ignorance into fields of possibilities.

Whether we've chosen to be professional sellers or to limit our sales experiences to everyday activities, such as cleaning out our attic with a garage sale or placing an ad on the community bulletin board to get rid of our old PC, knowledge of sales is a worthwhile investment. If we want to have control over what we have and how we use it, we need to get past the unwarranted fear of this business of buying and selling.

The knowledge of sales and the application of good sales attitudes and techniques have given me a wonderful career and earned me not only an excellent income but also, I believe, respect within the business community. Applying the same principles and behaviors to my personal life has helped me raise two lovely daughters and has brought me long lasting and deeply satisfying friendships. Sales has been very, very good to me, and *I am not a scary person.*

So in a few short pages we've dispelled all the nasty rumors about sales and sales people. Except for an occasional run-in with a few bad apples, every sale is honorable, and all sales people are charming, respectful, witty, warm hearted, and loving human beings. Perhaps I've gone a bit too far. At least we're not scary.

CHAPTER EIGHT

Listen Up!

"No one ever listened himself out of a job."
Silent Cal Coolidge, 29th President, United States of America.

"No one ever listened himself out of a sale."
Me.

S ELLING BEGINS AND ENDS with good listening. Before we begin the search for our first job or our first sale, we need to learn how to listen. Do you really listen, or do you wait to talk?

The purest listening we experience occurs in the presence of babies between the ages of two months and six months. They are old enough to have a feel for what's available and to understand what they want. They are not old enough to think about how to respond to what you say, because they don't understand the words you are saying, and they don't know how to talk. How, then, do they communicate? Take advantage of any opportunity you may have to observe babies.

Notice the countless expressions that cross their faces as they listen. When you approach a baby there will be a puzzled crinkling of his forehead and eyebrows, and a wait and see look in his eyes. If he knows you, he will recognize your voice before he recognizes your look. He will smile when he hears a familiar, soothing sound. If the sound is unfamiliar or if it changes, his expression will change. If the voice is harsh, his smile will disappear. A loud noise will make him jump. He may cry.

Watch the rest of his body. He will turn his head to noise. His legs and feet will start to kick, his arms will wave. He doesn't hide his reactions. You will know immediately that he is listening and he hears.

His parents' listening skills sharpen. They soon learn the difference between cries of hunger, cries from pain, and cries for attention. It's the same basic racket in all three instances, but with different inflections that require different responses. While his parents learn to answer his noisy needs, he learns to anticipate their responses and will reproduce the noises that bring the most desired reactions.

All this communication is going on and one participant doesn't know how to talk. Think about the possibilities of your getting anything done without a verbal exchange. The parents and their baby communicate by listening with heightened awareness of the tone of a sound, the look of a facial expression, and the perceived emotions of body language. Learn to listen with more than your ears.

An excellent group exercise to test your listening skills is to spend an hour or two with friends or colleagues and practice communication without language. Eat a meal or play a game and throw in a penalty whenever a real word is spoken. How well this works depends on how much you care about the outcome, so make the penalty count.

How well it works depends on how much you care about the outcome. Remember that. Embed it into your brain. Caring is the key to any endeavor, but it holds especially true when it comes to effective listening. The best, most successful sellers are those who truly care about their client's success as much as their own. It's easier to listen well when you care. It's the empathy factor.

Lest you think I've turned soft with suggestions that you spend your time observing babies and learning to truly care, please be assured the recommendations come from years of experience and pragmatic observation. The suggestions have a profitable track record. And I didn't say you have to care about the people you listen to. You only have to care about the outcome.

But there are other good reasons to care:

✦ You could hear your client's reasons to buy and learn what features to emphasize.

✦ You may hear an interest in more than one product, and selling two products is twice as good as selling one product.

✦ You will eliminate price as an issue because you will hear basic needs, and they are priceless.

✦ You will eliminate 90% of your competitors, who neither care nor listen.

✦ You may gain insider knowledge you can use on another buyer in the same industry.

✦ You could learn what people do outside of work and please them in ways you wouldn't have considered. For example, you learn that your buyer does volunteer work with the zoo and you create a promotion around the zoo designed to sell his product into the zoo gift shop. You not only deliver him a new customer but you also touch a personal hot button. Emotion is the element that triggers most decisions to buy. Emotions also last longer than apathy. Repeat business anyone?

✦ You could care about yourself. If you listen attentively, you could hear the price your customer is willing to pay for the product you are offering. You could make a sale that will pay you enough commission to buy you the new car you wrote down as one of your goals.

✦ If you no longer have reasons to not care, you could learn to really care, and your life will become much simpler.

We entered this world armed with an inherent capacity for listening. If you've misplaced that capacity, find it and recapture it. Practice listening every day with all your senses on alert. I cannot stress enough the importance of listening well.

If you can't listen, you can't sell.

A good listener: **Listens for more than words**. A good listener listens to understand. If you do not understand what the person is saying, ask for clarification. Don't be afraid to say, "I'm sorry. I don't understand. Could you explain that?"

Paces his listening to the customer's order and time frame. People speak at different speeds. If the speaker is talking slower than you'd like, don't leap ahead with assumptions. Slow down your listening speed, or you won't hear what the speaker is saying. You will hear words that aren't being said and you won't hear words that are being said. Don't leap ahead, for the same reasons. Assuming what the speaker is going to say is listening only to your own head.

Observes the other person's body language to determine the level of response. A yes, for instance, should be forthright and easy. If you hear yes and see a shrug, or if you hear yes and see eyes look away, you're not hearing yes. You're hearing maybe. Hold off on a decision until the body follows the voice.

Pays attention to the other person's tone of voice. How many ways can you say no or yes?

As in body language, the tone of voice indicates the level of response. If a yes, or a no, sounds like maybe, it is not a signal to move forward. It signals caution. Move ahead slowly and carefully.

Maintains objectivity. Refuse to allow personal feelings to affect what you are hearing. Hear it straight. Leave personal feelings and prejudices outside the room.

Notice that a good listener uses more than his ear. Just like babies, all senses contribute to the art of good listening. Stay tuned with your ears, eyes, and antennae.

A poor listener: **Picks on detail.** If a comment is irrelevant to the main idea, let it slide. Trivia is fun in a game at a party. Leave it there.

Offers unsolicited opinions. The listener should be seeking to hear information and opinions. You do not receive either one by filling the air with your own words.

Is subjective. Do not bring personal feelings into the room, and *never argue with a client.*

Is easily distracted. If a bird flies into the room and drops something on your shoulder, keep right on listening.

Be an active listener. It is the biggest time management system you have. If you hear with all your senses, you will not have to go back and ask for information to be repeated. You will not have to repeat work you've done incorrectly because you acted on information that you heard wrong. Do yourself and the important people in your life a big favor. Listen up!

CHAPTER NINE

Company Choices

Now that you know who you are and why you're in sales,
it's time to step up to the plate and hit one out of the infield.
Where are you going to work?

Y OU CAN'T SUCCEED in the workplace without having a
place to work. How's that for stating the obvious? First,
you need to decide what kind of arena you want to work
in. There are four obvious choices, having to do with the size of
the arena. This is a critical decision. You are looking for the place
where you will have your best opportunity for personal success.
You are looking for the place where you will do your best work.
Your choices are: **Large Corporate Company, Small Company,
Midsize Company, Home Office**.

Large Corporate Company

✦ There are more rules and regulations in a large company.
There has to be. The more people there are, the greater the
need to establish order. The variety of tasks and the necessity
for interdepartmental cooperation makes uniformity of attitudes and operations more essential in a large company than
in a small workplace.

✦ There are fewer personal options. For example, flextime is less likely to be allowed in a large company. The Department of Labor keeps a watchful eye on employee work schedules. Permitting the scheduling of work hours outside the standard eight hours a day, five days a week would be a paperwork nightmare. Allowing people to work some days at home is also not likely to be an option. Again, it's numbers. What a few can do, many cannot. Keeping track of who's in and who's at home would be a full-time job in itself and a frustrating exercise for co-workers and customers.

✦ There will be more opportunities for documented growth in a large company.Because everything tends to be clearly spelled out in large companies, goals are easier to establish and complete. You climb the ladder by acquiring titles, so each title can serve as a goal. Each goal becomes a check mark on your way to becoming president. One of the benefits of sales, you will recall, is the opportunity to move up.

✦ You will meet more people and have a broader spectrum of social access. While the corporate culture will dictate similarities in the comfort zones of a group structure, the sheer numbers of people available to you will offer a wider variety of people to know outside of work. Also, as your titles change, so will the group of people working with you, offering you even more opportunities for social interaction.

✦ The products offered by a large company have name familiarity. It's easier to get the doors of prospective customers to open if they recognize the name of the company and understand the uses and applications of the products. It's also easier to conduct personal business when you have a title with a company that loan officers recognize. And lastly, your family will breathe a sigh of relief knowing you are well situated in a career that offers the stability of largeness.

✦ There is a certain amount of anonymity in working for a large company. You can conduct your part of the business with less fuss as to how you are conducting it. If you are doing a good job, there are no bells and whistles. If you occasionally screw up, no whip lashes. Managers are spending their time sitting in conference rooms going over spreadsheets. They don't have time to micromanage.

✦ If you like to work on your own in a predictable atmosphere, with the security of someone else taking the risks and putting money into health care and retirement accounts, do your prospecting in the large company arena.

Small Companies

Nearly everything that's been said about large companies will be different from what will be said about small to midsize companies. There is a difference between small and midsize and the difference makes for confusion in the definition of how things are done and by whom. Let's begin with small.

✦ While federal and state regulations need to be clearly posted and given to employees as part of their hiring informational packet, that is as close as you will get to rules. The small company will have its own culture, but it is stated more in observable behavior than in written documents. You will need to pick up clues through your own sense of empathy as to how to conduct yourself in a small company.

✦ There are fewer positions in a small company. Area of responsibility is a more accurate way to describe tasks than actual titles. He's in sales, or she's in programming, or they take care of watering the plants, are phrases that describe departmental work distribution. Specific positions are more often multi-task than in large companies.

✦ There is a group mentality that's fun to be a part of, if you happen to agree with and enjoy the mentality. In a large company, people notice the car you drive but are less concerned with which lever you pull in the voting booth. In a small company they want to know which lever. If you vote for logging and they vote for the spotted owl, the atmosphere could get dicey.

✦ There is less privacy in a small company. Everyone knows how you are performing your work tasks and whom you are seeing on your lunch hours. You are expected to announce your baby's first tooth and an audit by the IRS. The atmosphere is more like family than you might like in a professional arena.

✦ Finding qualified customers is more difficult when you're working for a small company. Selling the products of a small company carries the initial disadvantage of having to explain at length who you are and what you are selling. You will also have to spend more time working on client service, keeping them assured that new, lesser known products can do as good a job for them as products produced by the big guys.

✦ Financial security and company benefits could be an issue, but it could be on the side of excellent as well as questionable. Small, family-owned companies that have been in business for many years take special care of their employees. They are loyal caretakers that will see you through both good and lean times. They understand the need for benefits and are careful to see that their benefit packages are competitive with large companies.

    Newer companies, on the other hand, may have trouble maintaining the costs of benefits and income growth. The primary goal of new companies is to return profits to the bottom line long enough to sustain the operation and growth of their business. They are building their own security and therefore, have less time for yours.

✦ If you enjoy feeling a part of a family or club that encourages input, validates your personal beliefs, and empathizes with your life struggles and successes, you will enjoy working for a small company. If you'd rather stick to work issues in an environment of personal privacy, look elsewhere.

Midsize Companies

Midsize companies can be difficult working environments. They have the qualities of both large and small companies and often appear schizophrenic in their goals and operations.

✦ Sometimes it's difficult to know what is expected of you, making it difficult to define their criteria for success. They often change goals and cultures as they seek to define their marketplace position. And when they make changes, they often change people. Job security can be a problem.

✦ Growing and maintaining market share is an all-consuming process. The possibilities of winning or losing as a company is a daily challenge. Big-time stress is a by-product of the struggles of midsize companies. Micromanaging is a given. Just as the company measures wins and losses on a daily basis, so will your performance be measured.

✦ Often the term midsize can apply to segments of a larger company. Media companies are a good example of this. Each radio and television station and each newspaper is part of a larger, more corporate company, but each one is run like a midsize company. If the parent lives in New York and the child works in Seattle, the differences in geographical cultures could create endless sources of friction. Are the differences really that great? The answer is YES.

Are there any benefits to working in this kind of atmosphere?

Well ... some people just get off on the highs and lows of conflicting cultures and daily stress. What can I say? It's radio and I have loved it, and, well, radio is like having an affair, rather than a marriage. Enough said.

Home Office

Working at home may sound like Eden, but while appearing to be idyllic, there are those tempting, red delicious apples lurking behind every garden path trying to distract you from the hardcore discipline required for making it on your own.

The Benefits

✦ You have flexible work hours. You can work fifteen hours a day or five hours a day, and you can work as many days as you want.

✦ You may focus on pursuing your own ideas and dreams.

✦ You can do everything your way, in the manner that suits your personal style.

✦ There is singular satisfaction. You can take all the credit you deserve.

✦ You can change direction without committee approval.

✦ You can do it for as long as you want to. No one will be taking your place.

The Hazards

✦ You have flexible hours. You will either work too much or too little. Be firm in your time allocations.

✦ The number of people needing your product, whether it is hard goods or a service, may not support your ideas and dreams. Carefully research the demand for your product so you will know the financial realities.

✦ Your preferred style of dress may only work while you are in your home office. The sweat suit may have to be abandoned when you go to market to peddle your wares.

✦ You aren't entirely free to do whatever you want. Your product and place of business may be subject to ordinances and regulations.

✦ You are responsible for providing your benefits and complying with government requirements. You pay for your own vacation time and your health care. You pay the employer share of social security, worker's compensation, and Medicare. You send in IRS payments monthly and file quarterly estimates. If you don't know how to and/or don't want to do these things yourself, you will have to hire a business manager or an attorney and CPA. In other words, you won't really be working by yourself.

✦ Singular satisfaction may give you the false impression that everything you do is wonderful. You need to actively seek feedback and opinions of other people to keep your product on the demand shelf.

✦ Can you really work in seclusion? You will be surprised how much personal interaction takes place every day in the outside world and how much you may rely on it. You may miss being among people. I make it a point to have lunch or dinner out two days a week when I've sequestered myself to get a project done. It refreshes my mind to have in-person conversations with other human beings.

* Changing direction without any input could cost you time and money. Set up consistent, periodic reviews with your clients to see if change is warranted. Don't rely completely on them, however. Clients are apt to resist change just because it's change. Also keep track of what competitors are doing. Clients, even if they resist change, don't like to feel they are missing out on new trends.

✦ Understand that as long as you have someone buying your product, you have a boss. No one is ever completely self-employed.

✦ You can keep at it too long and too hard. Keep a perspective on your work. Make sure you also have a life.

✦ Because you are singularly responsible for both results and rewards, you are vulnerable to the temptations of ego, obsession, and sloth.

Oh dear. There are more hazards than benefits in working out of your home office. But numbers don't tell the whole story. Benefits could still outweigh hazards. If the taste of the apple is worth the risk of temporary setbacks, venture into the garden.

There Is Another Choice

Companies in Transition

If you are a real glutton for punishment, and if you have an extra dose of patience and self-esteem, you might choose to go to work for a company in transition. They consist of small companies, midsize companies, and large companies all getting bigger, if they are the buyers, or becoming a smaller part of a big company or going away completely, if they are being bought.

Mergers, buyouts, or as some people call them, "consolidations," are back. The mergers of the 1980's, the egocentric decade of excess, were less than rip-roaring successes. Many large and powerful companies have spent nearly a decade eating crow while they attempt to regain the market positions they held prior to their ill-advised acquisitions. Why do we think today's mergers will be different? The wisdom of hindsight? The teachings of history?

I don't see evidence of that. The consolidations taking place today appear to have all the ego-driven mistakes of the past.

1. They have no clear definition as to why they are buying and selling, other than to say, "the other guys will if we don't" or "you have to be big to survive."

    The other guy will what? Lose money? Lose net percentages? Define big. What level of acquisition makes you a world player, and if you're not a world player, are you big enough to take the risk of acquisition?

2. There is no long-term planning, only long-term ideas. "We're going to buy those guys and get big." And then what? Hire more people? Where are you going to put them? Expand current product lines, or buy and sell new products?

3. They make knee-jerk decisions based on the demands of new levels of debt, rather than thoughtful decisions based on steady, long-term growth. Sales departments are given unrealistic goals based on company debt rather than market dynamics and sales development. Sales departments are not given new or increased backup tools to achieve higher goals. Cutting expenses becomes more important than increasing revenues, and revenue growth is often impeded.

4. Everything is short term. There is no loyalty from either the company or the people on the line. People are fired to cut company expenses, or they jump ship for ridiculously small sums of money because they feel (justifiably?) insecure in the new environment.

5. Management acts as if it is business as usual even though the business has changed dramatically. I don't know if they are pretending because they know that something has changed but they don't know what, or if they really believe that nothing has changed.

The people on the line believe that everything has changed! And they are all very much afraid of what is going to happen to them.

This is what you walk into when you choose to work for a company in transition. Because of forced layoffs and personnel defection, there will be job opportunities, and if you prove your mettle, there will be a fast track to promotions. I would not recommend a company in transition as a career choice for newcomers to the business world. It's for the seasoned risk takers.

You now have five choices from which to choose your career site. Select the arena in which you believe you will succeed. Your first official sale is coming up.

CHAPTER TEN

Your First Official Sale

*You understand by now that you've been selling all your life,
so we can't call this next step your first sale. We have to call it
your first "official" sale, because it's the first time you've decided
in advance that someone is going to buy your product.*

THIS SALE IS GOING TO HAVE a familiar ring to it. Your first official sale is going to be the same as my first official sale. You're going to sell yourself into a sales position, at a company of your choice. The best way I know to do this is to develop a questionnaire that will put you where you want to be.

There are two questions you need to answer before you direct any inquiries to someone else: **What kind of environment do you want to work in? What kind of product do you want to sell?**

What kind of environment do you want to work in?

1. Do you want to work in a: a) large corporate company?
   b) small company?
   c) midsize company?
   d) home office?
   e) company in transition?

List 8 companies in the category you selected. Answer the questions that follow, for each company you've listed. If you've chosen to be self-employed in a home office, follow the next steps as if you were looking for employment with someone else. The questions still need to be answered.

2. What is the company logo or philosophy? This will give you an idea of its goals and work ethic.

3. How many years has the company been in business? This will establish stability and allow you to check out its reputation.

4. How many locations and how many employees? This will give you an idea of your growth potential inside the company.

5. How much access will you have to your manager? How many managers?

6. What kind of team will you be joining? How many salespeople?

7. What kind of research and creative support will be available to you?

8. What are the work hours and the number of required meetings?

9. How are client lists assigned?

10. What kind of benefit package does the company offer?

What kind of product do you want to sell?

Products will be discussed in more detail in the next chapter. Give simple, gut-level reactions for now.

1. Tangible? This means hard goods, such as cars, home appliances, and real estate. List 8 products that would interest you.

2. Intangible? This means ideas and promotions, such as media sales, health services, and concerts. List 8 products that would interest you.

3. Big ticket or small ticket? Do you want to work several weeks or months to sell one or two products, or would you rather have a sale every day? Put the word "big" or "small" after each tangible or intangible product you listed.

4. Does the product have many competitors, like soft drinks and cars, or is it more exclusive and personal, like real estate and specific training courses?

5. What is the average unit price of the product and how many units are available for you to sell? Ask how many units the current sellers process in a month's time.

6. What is the compensation package - base pay plus commission, or draw against commission? What is the commission rate? Do they pay you on billing or delivery?

   Sit down, take out your calculator, and see if the number of units processed per month, times the commission rate will give you the monthly income you want.

   U x UP x CR = MI

   (100 Units x Unit Price of $1,000 x .05 Commission Rate = $5,000 Monthly Income)

7. How much money are the current sellers making, and how long have they been working there?

You have your questions written down, and you have a solid idea of what kind of company you want to work for and what kind of product you want to sell. Get as many questions answered as you can by personal investigation, prior to taking the next step.

The next step is to contact the Human Resources person for the companies who fit your criteria and ask for a listing of job openings. If there are none, depending on your level of interest, either ask for a job application or cross the company off your list.

Select six companies and formalize your goals and qualifications in a resume directed toward these companies. Each resume will be an original copy and personal, *mentioning the name of the company in the resume.* This small detail will distinguish you from other applicants.

Employers look for a few basic points, well stated, and written on *one piece of paper.* They want only what is relevant to what they are looking for, so pick *one job per company.* Do not attempt to hedge your bets and apply for several positions within the same company. Sales Managers want Sellers; Promotions Managers want Promoters; Marketing Departments want Marketers. If you apply for all of the above positions, they will think you consider yourself *sort of* qualified for *something* and *not really qualified* for *anything,* to say nothing of your desperation to take any job available. *You want a position in Sales, and you are willing to wait for the right opportunity.*

Resume

Name in bold type
(So interviewer can see at a glance, in case he forgets)
Address
Current phone number

CAREER OBJECTIVE: One sentence, specific job.

SUMMARY OF QUALIFICATIONS: Make it clear that you understand the job and have the necessary personal and professional qualifications to do the job.

EDUCATION: No nursery school, grade school, or junior high. High school, college, if you have it (and you should have it), trade school, and specific training seminars relative to the job. List no more than five educational experiences.

EXPERIENCE: Don't list everything you have ever done, or describe jobs in detail. Most employers understand what a supply sergeant, sales manager, personnel director, or choirboy does. If the potential employer does not know the experience you have listed, you may explain it in your interview.

INTERESTS AND ACHIEVEMENTS: All else being fairly equal, this is the tiebreaker. Community interests and professional achievements look good. But so do sports, travel, etc. Anything you do or have done to make you a more interesting person will be to your benefit. No more than four lines, however.

It helps if there is an experience, interest or achievement that will tweak some curiosity. Like a 250-pound defensive tackle who reads Shakespeare (I hired one), or a year of study in the Amazon. I had two candidates once who were deadlocked as far as professional qualifications. I picked the one who played the fiddle for fun. Why not?

Follow up with the companies you selected to receive your resume. Call and ask for an appointment. It's not difficult to get an appointment for a job interview. Good companies generally have a policy of interviewing a certain number of job applicants per quarter. (Tip: The last month of a quarter some managers may be playing catch-up and will be more available for interviews.) The policy began as an Equal Employment Opportunity requirement and may be continued for that reason, but it's just good business on the employer's part to have a list of qualified prospects available, in case a new position becomes available or a vacancy occurs in an existing position.

Here is how the phone conversation might sound:

"This is Robin Smith. May I speak with Mac Johnson, please? I am following up on a letter he received from me last week."

"Mr. Johnson. This is Robin Smith. Robert Wilson suggested I give you a call. I'm very interested in pursuing the possibility of working for you. You should have received my resume last Wednesday or Thursday. I'm available to meet with you next Monday or Tuesday morning."

Wait for his response and if you can accommodate him, agree to his time schedule.

That ought to get you the appointment. Set at least four interviews per week. Make the job that is least likely to transpire your first interview, so you can practice your skills before you are on stage to interview for the position you really want. Schedule no more than one interview per half day. You will want to evaluate each interview as soon as it is completed and be mentally and emotionally fresh for the next meeting.

You are well on your way to finding yourself a place to work.

✦ CHAPTER 11 ✦

Mentors and Other Helping Hands

For all our bravado in pursuit of independence and self improvement, it helps to have people helping us.

ARLIER, I MENTIONED MY TWO HEROES, Barbara Jordan and Stephen Hawking. Both faced physical liabilities. More than likely, neither the late charismatic Congresswoman from Texas nor the cosmologist from England was given the remotest chance of living their incredible lives, lives that have so greatly contributed to the enrichment of the growth and understanding we have of our society and our universe. There are others who come to mind. Jim Abbot could have looked in the mirror, seen only one arm, and thought he could never become a baseball player, much less pitch a no-hitter in a Yankee uniform. Albert Einstein was a sickly little runt who did poorly in elementary school. Their Mirror Images stunk, but their Gut Checks negated all of their perceived handicaps.

I can't say that I spend my days reflecting on the accomplishments of these people. But I keep them, and all the millions of quietly courageous people who have overcome difficulties, in the back of my mind to give my personal gut check a jolt whenever I begin to think I am somehow put upon or less gifted than I'd like to be.

The fact is, I am not gifted in any outstanding way. On my own, I can't think of a single accomplishment I could chalk up as being remarkable. But with the presence and assistance of a number of people, I can say I've done pretty well. My support staff—my **Helping Hands**—has seen to that.

We have our **Personal** helping hands. My daughters, Rebecca and Shannon, are my Number One personal hands. The courage, commitment, and empathy they've shown toward their mother's untested and unschooled childrearing faux pas and outright blunders have seen me to my greatest life accomplishment, which is - them. The negotiating skills and character expansions we learn from our children are invaluable.

I have also been blessed with friends who give me unconditional support that fortunately does not preclude the dishing out of pointed advice now and then. A few yes- men in our lives boost our egos when we need a quick fix, but they don't give us a true picture of who we are and where we need to be. We also need people who have the pluck and insight to call a butt head a butt head. Being more than a little headstrong, I've allowed only a few people in my entire life to get away with that, but they are an important few people, and I'm a better person for having allowed them their honesty.

In addition, I have **Professional** helping hands on all levels. Early in my professional career, there was the important boss, Fred Kaufman, whose approach so matched my father's low key, man-of-few-words posture that I could instantly follow his lead. He gave me two sentences that were so simple and so direct that I'll never forget their impact on my professional career.

"I was wondering if you were going to make a move," he said, in our first conversation about my making the move into sales. That told me he'd been watching me and believed in my potential. His quiet manner was so different from the salesperson examples I'd seen, and he was so respected and successful, I felt his confirmation of my potential was nearly a guarantee of my success.

"We're in this for the long haul," was the second statement he made that stayed with me. It meant that he considered my deci-

sion to be a career move, not just a step to greater income potential until a man came along to fully support me. At the time it was
a very important statement. It also meant that he was in it for the
long haul *with* me. He would have to train me and cover my inexperience until I could become a major producer for the team. His
willingness to do that gave me back-up courage.

Most of my colleagues were helpful and supportive. Some were
not. Most of my assigned clients were helpful and supportive.
Some were not. Most of my support staff people were helpful and
supportive. Some were not. The point here is that not everyone
has the time or the inclination to give us helping hands. We need
to discern who will and who won't.

Not only will some people not help, some will actually want you
to fail, and they are more than willing to assist you with a push in
that direction. Negative assistance can come from two directions.
One direction will be **Frontal Duck Bites** and the other will be
Brickbats from Behind. Frontal Duck Bites can be irritating, but
they are overt so you know they exist and can choose how you
want to deal with them. Brickbats from Behind can be lethal,
because they often come from people who appear to be helping
hands. You don't know you have a problem. They can gain a
foothold before you know what's happening.

Duck Bites are fairly harmless. They are people who are envi-
ous of your success. Their attacks are a reflection of their frustration with themselves for not having the mettle to be where you
are. You can ignore them, and they will continue their annoying
but mostly ineffectual ways. Or you can try to win them over to
your side by making them helping hands, praising them loudly
and often, letting them and everyone around them feel that you
wouldn't be where you are if it weren't for them. If they turn their
attitude around and show ability for growth, some day you may
become their helping hand.

Brickbats are dangerous. They want something, and very often
what they want is what you have, either your position or your
special person. If there are brickbats in your life, move swiftly
and firmly to put a stop to their behavior. No whining and no gos-

siping. Tell one confirmed ally what you suspect and let that person help you to confirm or deny your suspicions. If confirmed, take the brickbat away from the setting of subversion and let him or her know, quietly and unequivocally, that you're onto their scheme and it will not work.

If it is a work brickbat, go directly to your supervisor and tell him or her that the brickbat's show of support is false and so are the bricks he's throwing. Make it clear to your supervisor that you are one hundred percent on her team and you consider the matter closed. Then go back to work as if nothing has happened. If your supervisor starts acting nervous around you and fails to show some form of support, you might consider a letter to Human Resources and a resume to a competitor. If it's a personal brickbat, go right to the source and suggest the possibility of a kneecap alteration.

Most people, in fact nearly all the people in your life, will be supportive and forthright. We needed to take care of those few who are not.

Now, as for those **Helping Hands**:

Four regulars are needed: **Personal Only, Personal Professional, Professional Managerial, Professional Subordinate**.

Personal Only: This person is aware that you have a professional life, but knows little about it. She only sees you interact with friends and family. She knows your personal history, and therefore knows where you are coming from if a small incident becomes the backbreaking straw. She has the courage to tell you when you're overreacting and to accept, though not support, your irrationalities. She also will tell you honestly when you need to change something that is not good for you, from your dangerous flirting with the tennis pro to the mealymouthed acceptance of your spouse's philandering. Stay away from enablers, whose support only helps you stay in a harmful, ongoing situation. Most of the time your personal only helping hand will only have to tell you to wear the purple dress or the charcoal and maroon tie. But choose someone who can give you more help, if needed.

Personal Professional: This person knows you lead a double life and can empathize with the problems of having two worlds, because he also lives in two worlds, although his working world is separate from yours. He understands that the two worlds may offer conflicting values occasionally and will help you to keep your worlds in balance. Also, by having a foot in the working world, but not in your working world, he can offer you insight as to generally accepted business practices. You will then have a feel for what problems may be universal versus those that may be unique to your situation.

Professional Managerial: This person is your mentor. She will be your teacher and your leader to upward mobility. By virtue of her position, encouragement and commitment are expected. The most important ingredients to look for are understanding and a compatible style. You must feel comfortable exposing your inexperience and vulnerabilities. She must be able to teach you both the business and the ropes, and to turn vulnerabilities into assets. While you work to establish your own personality and abilities, your mentor's characteristic similarities will be demonstrating to you that the image you have of success will work. This gives you the courage to borrow from it and add personal touches along the way. Be careful not to overburden your mentor with all your enthusiasms and needs. It's a fine line between having her help you on your road to success and becoming a pest. Keep in mind that she has a full-time career of her own.

Scheduling monthly updates the first year is a good guideline. One half hour is sufficient. Come prepared with a specific point of discussion. Once a quarter, offer to buy lunch. Select an upscale restaurant. It never hurts to be seen lunching with a person whose station is a step above yours. If an emergency comes up, you should feel comfortable making an unscheduled call, but make sure it's an emergency.

Professional Subordinate: The most important link in the corporate ladder is your assistant. There is a very tight pipeline in the world of support staff, and you want to be in the loop. They know more about the bowels of the corporation than you could ever hope to learn on your own. Treat your assistant with respect and allow him his privacy. Don't ask him to betray confidences. Take him to lunch at important places on days other than his birthday, Secretary's Day, and Christmas. Unexpected personal notes of thanks are also effective strokes.

Be cognizant of his workload. Allow enough lead-time for special projects. He is not your errand boy. Do your own banking and shopping. If he's busy, make your own copies and send your own faxes. Let him know that while you would not respect his telling you confidential or personal information, you would like to know what is going on and be given a feel for the atmosphere on any particular day. You also want to know when "surprise" visitors may drop into the office, so you'll be ready in your best corporate suit on top of your suit of armor.

Helping Hands are an invaluable source of knowledge and know-how. You will require more than your own talent and energy to succeed. Having the right team of people who can cultivate your assets and create a few lucky breaks when you're prepared to take advantage of them is often the only point of difference that moves you ahead of equally talented people in the pursuit of brass rings. If you've chosen your helping hands wisely, they will be flattered by your calling on them and pleased to help you grow. It's a compliment to their accomplishments.

Have two Helping Hands in place before you make your major career decisions. Your **Personal Only** and your **Personal Professional** helping hands can help you to sort out the job options and select the right environment for your particular skills and personal strengths. While the ultimate decision will be yours, you should seek help with the sorting and coordination of information.

You are going to have to find helping hands on your own, even in the workplace. The traditional apprenticeship programs that offered a great resource of training for career recruits are nearly nonexistent in today's working world. Forced retirements, through the offering of golden parachutes to make room for the next generation, and questionable downsizing to bring in the current bottom line, have put the onus of training on managers who, more often than not, haven't the time, inclination, or experience to fill the void of the missing mentors. The **Professional Subordinate** shouldn't be that difficult to bring on board. The right **Professional Managerial** may be more elusive. Begin your search as soon as you arrive.

As you climb your own ladder to personal and professional success, make yourself aware of opportunities you may have to assist or mentor others. Offer your hands to the very worthy and much needed investment of helping people grow. You will begin to understand the satisfaction the people you've chosen to be your helping hands feel for having given you a firm but gentle push toward greater rewards.

The fulfillment I receive in observing the outstanding performances of professionals who began their careers under my tutorage is second only to the incredible feeling I have when I find myself in the awesome presence of my remarkable daughters. It is the ultimate high.

CHAPTER TWELVE

The Three Elements of a Sale

*Sales is the buying and selling of goods, services, and ideas.
It's a simple concept and it doesn't necessarily cost money.*

A NUMBER OF DIFFERENT FACTORS go into a sales undertaking, but three elements are present in every sale: **The Product**, **The Buyer**, and **The Seller**.

The Product

There are two kinds of products: **Tangible** and **Intangible**.

Tangible products have specific components that the buyer can see, touch, and measure. A solid oak dining table in a contemporary design that seats eight is a tangible product. A blue mini-van that gets thirty miles per gallon and seats six is a tangible product.

Tangible products, for the most part, are easier to buy and sell than intangible products. First, there is a need, real or imagined, on the part of the buyer. Second, the buyer knows what the need looks like.

You have nothing to pull a chair up to at dinnertime. You need a dining table that matches your chairs, and because it will match your chairs, you know what it's going to look like. Your family has outgrown the small green sedan that seats four. You have to buy a larger vehicle. You want a mini-van and you'd like to try a new color. Let's try blue this time.

Our buyers have determined their needs and pictured them in their minds. They are ready to buy. All they have to do is find the product, which matches the one they imagined, and figure out a way to pay for it. Some seller, somewhere, is going to get to sell an oak dining table, and some seller, somewhere, is going to sell a blue mini-van. The buyers are going to walk into their showrooms. This would appear to be a done deal for the seller. What could possibly go wrong?

The buyer doesn't have to buy from a *particular* store or seller. The person who's buying the van, for instance, wants to make a good investment. Mini-vans are available for sale at a number of different places, with a wide range of options and at various price levels. The buyer wants to shop around. She's done her homework. She knows what the factory has to offer. If she's a smart buyer she will spend just as much time researching the factory dealerships as she has spent on product options. The dealerships house the sellers, and the sellers make the deals.

The seller doesn't have to bother with all the options of the buyer. He has a specific product line and a price range set by the owner of the dealership, with factory input. All the seller has to do is sell himself. He, personally, is the make or break factor in this sale. The buyer knows what product she wants. She has yet to make up her mind about who's going to sell it to her.

The buyer walks into the showroom. The seller approaches her. She is sizing him up, looking at how he is dressed, noticing how he carries himself, and checking the expression on his face. *I wonder if I can trust this guy,* she's thinking. *He looks okay,* she decides, *and his greeting is pleasant enough.* He has just passed her first run through. She could have said, "Just looking, thanks." But she is going to go to the next step and tell him what she's looking for. He says he has exactly the mini-van she wants.

The product will be sold. The buyer has already made the decision to buy. There will be a sales transaction and we're getting closer to knowing who will complete the sale. But this is her first stop. *Maybe I had better take this nice and easy*, she says to herself. *This is going too fast.* What seems to be a certain sale could be lost if the seller tries to rush her, but he doesn't know that yet. He's going to have to notice her hesitancy as he reads her body language. Can he do it? Everything seems perfect. Will he lose the sale just because he's the first stop along the way? Any number of factors could influence the buyer's decision to purchase *this* product from *this* person at *this* place of business. Who knows if this deal is going to gel? There's always a sliver of uncertainty, even in a slam-dunk.

Intangible products are more difficult to buy and sell. Potential buyers can't see or touch them. Sometimes they don't even know they are in the market to buy or that the product exists. There is no established need to buy and therefore, no bank of buyers looking for a place to throw down their money. First, the sellers have to find potential buyers. Then they have to sell them something they have no perceived need to buy.

I sell radio advertising—air. It's an intangible product. Wanna buy some air? Har har. What I do is considered a joke in some circles and a personal affront in others. Nobody needs to buy radio advertising. It pains me to say this, but there actually are thriving, successful businesses that have never bought radio advertising. Is it possible that some of them would be more successful if they were to raise their visibility by buying radio advertising? I certainly think so. But there are very few buyers knocking on my door to prove me right. Once in a while a business will actually call a radio station and ask to talk to someone about buying an ad or two, but for the most part, radio sellers have to find potential buyers and suggest that they can fill a need the buyers don't know they have. That's infinitely more difficult than demonstrating a product to someone who's already made a decision to buy.

I see health care facilities advertising on television. Their message is addressing *anticipated* needs, or the *prevention* of anticipated needs. And if that isn't enough of a buyer turnoff, make the anticipated need a *dreaded* need. "If you should have symptoms of a heart attack...." Try getting that message across in a thirty-second sound bite before the buyer heads to the kitchen for beer relief.

These are complicated sells, so complicated that three groups of sellers pool their own needs and resources to find a way to anticipate what will capture the attention of their potential buyers' anticipated needs.

1. There are people who sell tangible products to the health care facility. Heart machines, prepackaged thermometers, etc. And there are people who sell intangible products to the health care facility. Post trauma counseling, systems coordination, etc.

2. There are people who sit on the health care facility's board of trustees who determine what product lines, tangible or intangible, will be emphasized and therefore, what kinds of buyers will purchase them. The board must predict which product will bring in the most buyers. It is the board's responsibility to see that the health care facility turns a profit.

3. After the board makes its product decisions, there are marketing and advertising specialists who are the experts in reaching the prospective buyers. The most difficult part of the three-part sales effort is in the hands of these experts. Quite often, the most sought after buyers do not want to need the products the health care facility anticipates they might need. Planned Parenthood clinics, with their much needed and often maligned services, come to mind as a particularly difficult product to sell. Can you think of others?

There is an unending supply of tangible and intangible products available to keep the buying and selling process going strong. It makes sense to learn about the people participating in the process.

The Buyer

You will meet the same kind of buyers regardless of which product you choose to sell. Most buyers are straightforward and need only the right product, the right price, and the right power of suggestion to make a purchase. But there are a few buyers who propose greater challenges to the seller. Three come to mind: **Eager, Anxious**, and **Detached**.

My personal favorite is Eager. Eagers have money and they want to spend it. OboyOboyOboy. If only we could spend all our time with Eager buyers. The problem is, we *could* spend all our time with the Eagers, unless we monitor our time carefully. One condition of taking Eager's money is that they take time - lots of time. Eagers are ego driven and they require mountains of service. Their behavior would cause people to believe they are sellers, which they usually are. But we are looking at them as buyers.

Eager buyers are guaranteed to have enough money to buy what you are selling. They've privately checked the tariff before inviting you to pitch. Their egos won't allow them to embarrass themselves by asking you to show your wares and then having to decline the purchase because they can't afford the price.

Most of the time you won't have to find Eager buyers. They will find you. They are a gift to sellers. They are the reward you get for spending weeks of your life cold calling to no good end. But good sellers don't wait around for the capricious phone to ring. Eager buyers can be found. It will cost you money, but you can find them.

◆ You can find Eagers in four-year colleges. Pay attention to your classmates. Hang out with the excellent students and the ambitious social climbers and stay in touch with them after you graduate. Or, if you wasted your college years with party people, keep in touch with your friends anyway. If you managed to grow up to be a responsible adult, chances are that some of your fellow goof-offs have matured as well. Contribute to the alumni fund and attend class reunions. Two of the most successful sellers I know have carried their college contacts into boardrooms.

✦ Eagers can also be found in the cultural arts. They donate time and dollars to the symphony, repertory theaters, and local art museums, sometimes because they enjoy them, and sometimes because they enjoy the recognition that comes with their donations. If you enjoy music, theater, or art, you might look here for your Eager buyers.

✦ Enter the sports arena. Play handball, play golf, play tennis. Buy season tickets. The best arenas for ticket hobnobbing are major league baseball and college football. It's expensive. Put a group together and divide the assets. My baseball group buys four season tickets to the Seattle Mariners. Each of us gets four tickets to twenty games, which gives us six months of captive client togetherness.

* Keep company with your parents and their friends. When you become a real adult, you will realize they are good people and they care about you. You will also realize they are an excellent source of introductions.

Now that you've found your Eager buyers, what do you do with them?

You sell them something that includes added value. You sell sizzle. They want to be recognized in their community. They want to rub elbows with celebrities. They want tickets on the fifty-yard line and box seats. They want their friends to have tickets. They want their sons and daughters to meet celebrities. They want to be heroes to people who are important to them. They want, want, and want.

I'm not making fun of Eager buyers. They're a great client find. They know what they want, they're fun and forthright, and they're willing to make decisions. You won't have to spend time uncovering needs or looking for hidden agendas. If you've got a product they like, they will buy all they can get of it. With so much of the business world made up of people who are passion protectors, the Eager buyer's zeal can be refreshingly intoxicating. Everyone needs one or two **Eager buyers**.

There is a downside, however, if you have a problem managing your time and resources. The Eagers will always ask for more. You will need to level a firm hand to keep them within the terms of their contract, and you must resist the urge to give them more time than you can afford to give. You have other clients and a life outside of professional sales.

There are additional potential problems. If you run out of goodies, or if someone else's goodies are bigger and better than yours, you may lose the Eager buyer. And, if they bought into a winning program that ceases to win, they may also jump ship. Passion runs its course and must be constantly renewed. In order to keep the Eagers from straying, you will have to make sure they are happy all the time and keep them thinking that what's to come is even better than what they have.

I sold a play-by-play sponsorship to the University of Washington Huskies football radio broadcasts to an Eager buyer. He happened to be a graduate of the dreaded cross-state rival, the Washington State Cougars, but he bought the Huskies sponsorship because they have a higher profile and historically have won more games. One year however, the Cougars not only beat the Huskies, but they also knocked them out of representing the PAC 10 Conference in the Rose Bowl. When the final Huskies' rally failed, Mr. Eager slammed down his program, said, "That's it!" and stomped out of the sponsor's suite. He did not renew his sponsorship and he refused to ever see me again because, as he told his front man to tell me, "The only thing I dislike more than losers, is people who sell losers." Oh well.

"Oh well" is the only response to have when that happens with an Eager buyer. It's a tough break, but another hit will come along to salve the ache of the drop in your commissioned income. It's far more serious when something like this happens in your personal life. Beware of the exhausting needs of the Eager in what you believe to be a long-term relationship.

Remember Scheherazade? She was the wife of a sultan of Persia who hated to be bored. He *really* hated to be bored. He chopped off the heads of people who bored him. Scheherazade managed to stay alive by telling such interesting serial tales nightly that the sultan kept her alive a day at a time, to hear the next episode. While few lose their heads for daring to succumb to occasional boring moments, many lose the relationships and the perceived good life they bargained for when they became too deeply involved with their eager friends, partners, and clients.

If life in the fast lane is what you want, then by all means go after it. Just keep in mind that it is a fragile and fleeting existence, unless you keep your foot on the *premium* gas pedal.

Anxious buyers are not nearly as much fun as Eager buyers are, but they have their assets. The first kind of Anxious buyer is ruled by *fear*. These are the buyers who are afraid of being sold. Their fear is that you will sell them something they don't want, or charge them too high a price for something they do want. They don't trust themselves to make wise decisions. Therefore, they don't trust you. This makes them anxious. Your job is to earn their trust by allowing them to come to a buying decision on their own. This takes time and it is not particularly fun, but your reward will come from the loyalty they will show you when you eventually win them over. Then they can be fun.

Once the transaction is complete, and the results prove it to be a good investment, the Anxious buyer will take credit for having made the correct decision to buy ("Bought it myself.") If you allow him to continue to make excellent decisions, you will earn commissions from him indefinitely. Internally he understands what you have contributed to his success and he is aware of your willingness to let him be the star. You have earned his trust forever.

If you should change jobs, the company you work for will lose the Anxious buyer to a competitor, or to wherever you go. Employers expect an experienced recruit to bring accounts to the company. As you negotiate your contract with a new employer, you can say with confidence that you will bring this Anxious buyer's account with you.

Oddly enough, the Anxious buyer, ruled originally by fear, may become your good friend. You've overcome his fears and replaced them with trust. Trust is the first step to lasting friendships. This is a nice side benefit of taking the time to carefully develop a sale.

Not all Anxious buyers will become life-long pals or reliable sources of long-term revenue. Some have developed a permanent case of distrust. They are unwilling or unable to satisfy their discomfort with the purchasing process. No matter how carefully you've orchestrated their decision to buy, they will always feel they've been duped because trust, even in themselves, is beyond their ken. They will begin to find fault with the sale soon after you've reached what you thought was a solid agreement. They will look for reasons to break the deal or get some of their money back, because: a) they don't like the product - wrong color, doesn't work, doesn't fit; b) they think they paid too much; c) they don't trust the seller. Only you can determine whether or not they are ultimately worth your time and trouble.

Another likely reason for an anxious buyer's discomfort is that he wasn't a real buyer. He was a *"just looking,"* who got caught by impulse. He didn't intend to make a purchase. But since he did, he is still just looking, this time for a face-saving way to get out of it. Being an impulse buyer myself, I can empathize with the predicament, but I've learned to either absorb the cash outlay or own up to my impulse and beg their forgiveness. A good seller will help the just looking buyer find a way out of the sale. Just-lookers eventually stop looking and start buying.

The most difficult buyer for anyone who loves the art of the deal is the **Detached** buyer. Whether you're selling the idea of buying a new car to your spouse... "What do you think, Honey? Do you like it?" ...or a multi-million dollar takeover plan, if the buyer doesn't care, it takes some of the luster out of the transaction. Even if you know you'll look fabulous behind the wheel of that new little red car, if Honey responds with an uninterested... "umm, well, if that's what you really want...," you're not going to get the same pleasure from buying it as you would with an enthusiastic response. You may decide not get the little red car, which may be exactly the goal your Detached buyer had in mind.

There are three kinds of **Detached** buyers: **Consensus**, **Fake**, **Hired Hand**.

The **Consensus** buyer does what the label implies. He will not make a decision on his own. He will poll every person he can possible think of by either leaving a voice mail or dropping off what you've given him with a scrawled note or comment, "Take a look at this. Tell me what you think." If he gets a response, that means he will take action. If he doesn't, he will take no action. He prefers the latter response.

The only way to secure action from the Consensus buyer is to either hound him for a decision so he'll go after the consensus he needs, or go around him and contact the people he sends his scrawled messages to. He won't like either tactic on your part, but he'll move the sale along to either get you off his back—the Consensus detached wants you to disappear—or to protect his position with his advisers. Since he does not want to act on his own, he can't afford to lose the people who form his consensus. He knows they eventually will stop giving advice if they perceive the advice does not provoke a course of action.

The Consensus buyer takes action only to preserve his status quo. He buys because that's his job and he gets paid to do it. He doesn't have to like it and neither do you. Do what you have to do to get the sale. Three good things will come from your pursuit.

1. You will meet his consensus team. They are the real decision makers. The fact that you know them will prompt Consensus to move your proposals to the top of the pile. He actually will like having you know them. He can dispense with your annoying presence faster.

2. You won't have to spend time servicing him. He doesn't care about what happens when he's through with his part of the business. You will want to service his consensus team. They will evaluate the success or failure of the sale.

3. If the sale was worthy, contract renewal will be automatic, by e-mail, regular post, or telephone, if he can pull it off.

Before you dismiss your need to know the Consensus buyer completely, he may be a good person to know. It may only be his job that fails to engage his interest. If this account is going to be a long-term relationship, you might want to discover what his interests are and cultivate a relationship outside his office. Common ground outside the office may improve the business relationship.

Now we come to the vilest of all creatures, the **Fake** buyer. Not willing to own up to the fact that she is not in a position to make decisions, she will lead you on a merry chase. The wasted effort on your part will last indefinitely, if she perceives that you live on hope rather than reality.

All inquiries lead to her. "Who makes the marketing decisions?" "I do." "Who makes the buying decisions?" "I do." "Who chooses the carpets?" "I do." "Who disposes of the trash?" Okay so she doesn't do trash. In the worst case, hers is an indefatigable power trip. In the best case, giving her the benefit of being born on the topside of a rock, she is being used by her supervisor to screen sellers. In either case, she is wasting your precious time.

You've done the required screening, and all roads assure you that you are dealing with the decision maker. You follow all the steps to a successful sale and you get nothing but stalls and evasions from this buyer. At some point you realize it's time to finish the sale. You decide that you are dealing with someone who is afraid to make a decision and you will have to make decisions for her. That's okay. This is a legitimate course of action. This is done.

You request a meeting. She agrees. She likes to hold meetings. You review all the steps you've taken up to this point and ask if she has any further questions. She will have questions because she is stalling. After answering all her questions again, and allowing a reasonable amount of time for her hemming and hawing, you quietly take out a contract and a pen. You sign the contract and place it and the pen across the table in front of the buyer. You wait for her signature to appear. If she signs it and passes it back to you, your patience has paid off and you pop some well-earned corks. She was only stalling because she enjoyed the attention she was getting from you in the process of buying.

If, on the other hand, she confesses that she does not have the authority to sign the contract, tell her you will wait at the table while she gets the person who does have the authority to sign. If she says that person is not available and you have far more patience than I do, you will ask for that person's name. If you sit in my circle of patience saturation, you will pick up the contract and the pen and walk out the door, and get the name from someone else. Your pride will not allow you to let her watch you pound your fists on your forehead in an ancient ritual of frustration. The other reason you walk out the door is so you will not lose your temper. NEVER lose your temper in front of a client or any person who has fed his or her ego by wasting your time and diminishing your enthusiasm.

Some Detached buyers don't mind signing contracts. They just want to do it in their own time, after they're satisfied that they've seen and analyzed all the possible facts relating to the sale. Their detachment is a learned behavior and it is a perfectly valid approach to the progression of the sale. I call them **Hired Hands**.

The seller must understand two things about the Hired Hand. First, he does not have a personal stake in the completion of the transaction. He will make the purchase based strictly on the need to buy as determined by the presentation of facts. Graphs, statistics, and bullet points will be assessed for their value to the point of sale. There is no need to discover his favorite sport or recording artist, or send birthday greetings to his son. Save the song and dance for a more interested audience.

Second, the Hired Hand is in no hurry to make the purchase. The seller will have to establish the time frame and get the buyer to agree to it. It won't be easy. The buyer will resist efforts to speed up the presentation or to close early. The seller must carefully plan the meeting so that every point is made and every objection is answered, ten minutes before the sand reaches the bottom of the hourglass. At that moment, the seller needs to stop talking and allow the buyer time to make a decision to buy ... or not to buy. Silence now gives the seller the edge. The buyer must respond. This is an important step in working with the Hired Hand. He is not uncomfortable with silence; that's his tactic. He may be surprised that you are borrowing his ploy but he will understand that the next move is his. If you break the silence, you will lose the sale, at least for this moment.

Certain cultures and geographic areas have more Detached buyers than others. With amusement, I've watched people from the East Coast of the United States trying to get a deal consummated in the Pacific Northwest. Doing business with the Pacific Rim may be a new buzz for the rest of the world, but we Nor'westers have been trading with the Far East for over a century. The basic premise for our mutual business discussions is "He who speaks first, loses." And the longer he speaks, the more he loses.

Eventually all real buyers will buy, because that is what they do. What products they buy and who they buy them from is in the hands of the seller. There is a real need for better sellers.

The Seller

There are as many different kinds of sellers as there are people who sell because, as we've learned, sellers sell themselves. For the purpose of discussion in this chapter, however, we're going to divide all of our individual selves into two groups. All the better to match products and buyers to sellers, my dear.

I alluded to left brain and right brain inclinations in the comparisons of industrialist traditions and computer innovations. Our brains are neatly divided into two hemispheres, looking top down. Individuals tend to use one side of the brain more than the other. We're either more prone to be left-brained or right-brained in the way we work and make decisions. I think it's interesting that most definitions of our two cerebral hemispheres happen to match the two primary kinds of products that are bought and sold.

Basically, the **left brain** processes the **tangible** brain duties. It is oriented toward statistics and tasks. The talents and inclinations of left-brain people lie in the gathering, arranging, absorbing, and solving of factual information. This is their comfort zone. This is what they do best.

The **right brain** processes the **intangible**. It is creative in nature and oriented toward ideas and feelings. The talents and inclinations of the right-brained person lie in brainstorming ideas and solving people's problems. This is their comfort zone. This is what they do best.

The left brain/right brain suggestion I am presenting here is based on scientific fact, a fact I feel we too often ignore in making personal and professional decisions. It is *particularly important* to know the natural inclinations of people who sell, because selling is an integral part of our total person. It is true that all sane people have equal access to both sides of the brain and use both sides to some extent, so we should be careful to avoid placing restrictive labels on mere inclinations. However, in sales we concentrate on going with our best opportunity for success. We call it our "best shot." Our best shots will come from our natural inclinations.

When I was in the first grade, schools tried to make everyone write with their right hands. No left-handed pens allowed. Educators relented only when psychologists were able to prove that this *unnecessary conformity* created scholastic havoc with left-handed school children. Denial of a natural inclination interfered with the education of many thousands of students.

To put a more modern spin on it, let's say all golf clubs will be right-handed, and everyone will use a two wood to tee off. To hell with your natural inclinations and throw away your best opportunity for shooting par. We want all golfers standing where they're supposed to, on the right-handed side of the tee. And all our employees will use the same club off the tee that our CEO uses. Never mind that she's 5'1" and her nine iron will only get her 115 yards, while you're 6'4" and the two wood will land you half way through the next hole. We want uniformity here. Everyone plays golf the same way. How far do you think that idea would fly?

1. Every product is the same

2. Every buyer is the same.

3. Every seller is the same.
   That makes no sense, on or off the golf course. Try this:

1. Every product that is sold can be positioned statistically or creatively.

2. Every product has many buyers. Some will want a car with eight cylinders to power a 5-litre engine that gets 22 miles per gallon. Others will want a roomy sedan in midnight blue with gray leather interiors. Same product, different buyers.

3. Every sales team can use both right brain and left brain sellers to sell their product to an endless assortment of buyers.

I don't want to oversimplify this right-brain/left-brain theory. It is far more complex than as described here, and I am no expert on the full range of its implications. I am using it to illustrate that there is a genetic basis for our inclination to be either analytical or creative in our problem solving activities, and I want to encourage you to recognize and develop your natural talent.

The buying and selling of goods and services is a simple idea made complicated by the vagaries of human nature. We cannot create a formula that will capture the possibilities of more than a billion different personalities. We can only anticipate tendencies we've observed over time. The challenge in any human undertaking is to simplify variety. *Simplify variety*. Let's make that the oxymoron of record for this book.

To summarize, **products** are basically either **tangible** or **intangible**. But every product has intangible qualities that can be highlighted to fulfill the needs of buyers who are looking for more than facts as they make their purchasing decisions.

Most **Buyers** are ready and willing to buy. Buyers buy. All they need is a well-positioned product to fit their purchasing requirements. It's the people we've labeled **Eager**, **Anxious**, and **Detached** that require a more concerted sales and service effort. They are the minority but they take up most of our time.

There is an infinite variety of **Sellers**. To simplify the variety, we divide them into two groups; those whose basic talents lie in the analytical left side of the brain and those whose basic talents lie in the creative right side of the brain. The key to *being* a seller is knowing yourself and understanding how to use your assets. The key to *managing* a seller is in learning how to assess his natural talents and help him to acquire the skills he needs to use them. Figure out where *your* basic talents lie and concentrate on developing them fully.

CHAPTER THIRTEEN

Developing a Client List

You're all set. You know what sales is, why you're a seller, what kind of seller you are, how to listen, and who your helping hands are. You may even have a job. Now, who are your potential customers and how do you catch their attention?

INDING PEOPLE TO TALK TO is called prospecting. You've already learned how to prospect and sell yourself into a job. Even though *you* are always the product you are selling, the manner in which you reveal the product is quite different when you are looking for a client after you've found your base of operations. The main point of difference is the focal point of your preparation.

✦ In prospecting for a job you ask yourself what you will want from them. You prepare a list of questions *for* them that will answer *your* needs.

✦ In prospecting for a client you ask yourself what they will want from you. You prepare a list of questions that will provide you with information *about* them so you can fulfill *their* needs.

Before you prepare a list of questions to ask the prospective buyer you need to determine who the buyer is.

Define the buyer:

To develop a profile of the person or company you believe will benefit from your products and services, you must ascertain the presence of certain factors.

✦ Look for product compatibility. The product you are selling needs to be a suitable demographic fit with the product your client represents. You don't sell beer to children, or sports bras as accessories to strapless ball gowns.

✦ Determine your compatibility with the personnel involved. Whenever possible work with people who have values and work habits similar to yours. There's no need to throw your traditional, private personality into a free-form think tank, if you can avoid it.

✦ You must be able to gain access to the person who makes the buying decisons. Without the real buyer, there is no real sale.

✦ The buyer should have the financial capability to purchase enough of your product to accurately measure the results of doing business with you. Can they buy enough product from you to realize a profitable return on their investment? You want them to be sufficiently pleased with the results to give you another order and/or a good recommendation.

✦ You need to make sure the buyer has marketplace stability, either through historical reference or a current credit rating. You want them to be in business long enough to sell your product to their customers. Unsold inventory will be a reflection on the worthiness of your product more than the ability of the customer to sell your product.

Put yourself in the client's shoes:

✦ Prior to making a call as a seller, visit the prospect's place of business *as a customer*. What you are looking for are revelations and assurances that may help you to help your client.

✦ Notice the facility. Is it easy to find, attractive, and well organized?

✦ Observe their customers. Get a clear picture of the prospect's current clients. Are *they* a demographic fit with your product?

✦ Observe the traffic flow. Visit more than one time, on different days, at different hours. Are there conspicuous differences in numbers or demographics?

✦ Talk to an employee to verify your personal findings, using phrases like, "It seems to me...blah, blah...Do my observations reflect your experience?"

✦ Talk to an employee to get a feel for the success of the operations and the temperament of the work atmosphere.

✦ Take note of the signage and advertising strategies. *Learn how they sell themselves and you will learn how to sell to them.*

I don't believe in cold calls:

I believe in informational calls. Do enough homework up front that you will have something specific to say when you pick up the phone or hand them a business card. You want feedback. The purpose of a call is not for them to discover you, but for you to find out something about them. *Every encounter must produce information.*

You're going to need more than one customer:

✦ You don't have time for what is called the "spray and pray" technique of random dialing. That's the outdated principle of calling anybody and praying that someone will say yes.

✦ Write down five business categories that seem to have a product that is compatible with what you are selling.
    Example: The product is coffee makers. The business categories are real estate offices, radio stations, mortuaries, law firms, and public schools. I bet you didn't list the same five that I did - let your mind run rampant. Or, get out the Yellow Pages and start in the middle under categories. (Everyone starts with A or Z.)

✦ List eight individual businesses in each category.

You now have forty prospects. The list should have come together quickly. If you can't quickly list forty people to call, you need to review the potential for your being able to sell the product.

Too much has been said about prioritizing:

It's really very simple:

✦ Through the process of qualifying potential prospects, the ones you keep are the ones you call. If you're not going to call them, don't keep them.

✦ Bunch your calls by category. Call all the mortuaries in one group of calls, radio stations in another, etc. Practice breeds comfort. Comfort creates flow. Flow is easy to follow. Your fifth call to a mortuary will be better than the first call. Take a break after each category to organize your notes. Look for similarities and develop a plan.

✦ Save your best prospects for last for the reasons stated above.

Your fifth call will be better than your first call; your fifth category of calls will be better than your first.

How to Call the Buyer

*Do not try to sell your product over the phone
to a new prospective buyer.*

The only thing you want to sell over the phone is an appointment. If the buyer's location is in the area, you want an in-person appointment. If their location is outside your marketing area, you want an invitation to send them information. Every contact you make is a sales contact. Make it count. Get what you need out of it.

Keep in mind:

1. Of the people you attempt to reach by telephone, you will never reach 33% of them.

2. Of the people you attempt to reach by telephone, 33% of them will treat you like a piece of garbage. They are jerks. Don't waste your time with them.

   You haven't a prayer of doing business with 67% of the people you call.

3. Of the people you attempt to reach by telephone, 33% of them *may* be remotely interested in what you have to say.

Schedule telephone time:

1. Set aside thirty to sixty minutes every day to make prospecting phone calls.

2. If you don't have a private office, find a private place.

3. Use the same place every day.

4. Don't get sidetracked and don't miss a day.

Adjust your physiology:

1. Separate yourself from what you were doing prior to calling time by at least ten minutes.

2. Get yourself mentally prepared for a non-visual conversation. Develop mental pictures of an in-person conversation, including positive body language.

3. Get your body comfortable. Sit in a comfortable chair.

4. Clear the desk of irrelevant paperwork. Have a clean tablet in place and a pen in hand.

Be organized:

1. Have ten people to call each day. Have a card for each person, that contains: Name of the decision maker
Company name and product
Address, phone number,
fax number, e-mail address

Know the language:

1. Think and speak in their terms. Learn a few of their industry buzzwords.

2. Practice using them. (*"What is the average turn on your shelf talkers?"*)

3. They may mean nothing to you. Understand what they mean to your client.

Get beyond the Gatekeepers:

1. Gain support of the support staff by being professional and polite.

2. Ask them to help you.

3. Be specific about what you need them to do.

Have a purpose and a plan:

Seller: "Good morning. May I speak to Harmon Hope, please?"

Assistant: "Who is calling please? May I tell him what this is regarding?"

Seller: "This is Warren Anderson. I'd like to speak to Mr. Hope about plans for your Anniversary Sale." (You're not trying to sell anything to the assistant or Mr. Hope. You want to talk to Mr. Hope about his sale.)

Assistant: "I'll put you through, Mr....?"

Seller: "Thank you. You've been very helpful. My name is Warren Anderson. And your name is..." Write down his name.

You have thirty seconds to procure Harmon Hope's interest: Open, Hook, Close

Harmon: "Hello. This is Harmon Hope."

OPEN

Seller: "Hello Mr. Hope. This is Warren Anderson. I'm calling about your Anniversary Sale. (Focus on the customer.) Are you planning to have as big an event as you had last year?" (Forces a response to the purpose of the call —not to you.)

Harmon: "Yes we are."

HOOK

Seller: "The purpose of my call, Mr. Hope (Use the customer's name often. Before the conversation is over, he'll think you know him), is to discover if I may be able to help you with your sale. My company, Promotion Enterprises, has a successful track record for working with companies like yours. We worked with (name of a similar business) on their Memorial Day sale. Their profits increased 20% over their previous year's sale."

CLOSE

"I'll be near your offices next Monday and Tuesday. Which day would be better for you?" (Eliminate the pressure of Mr. Hope being the only reason for your visit to his neighborhood.)

Harmon: "Tuesday is good for me."

Wasn't that the easiest thing you've ever done?

Overcome objections

1. There are, on average, three objections per phone call.

2. Keep track of the objections you get and responses that work.

3. Use scripts or reference sheets. No one will see your cheat sheets.

4. Find a way to agree with or reassure the objector.

5. Handle objections quickly and **move on**.

OBJECTION	**POSSIBLE RESPONSE**
No.	That might be a good decision. But let me ask.... Is there a reason you said no?
I don't have time to talk to salespeople.	That's understandable, since we've not had an opportunity to get acquainted. It sounds to me like that's final. Is that the case, or shall I call back at a better time?
I'm not the person you should talk to.	No problem. Would you be kind enough to tell me whom I should be talking to?
I don't have time today.	It sounds like I've hit you at a bad time. Could you tell me when it would be more convenient for me to call?

The first few times you pick up the phone could be a little unnerving. Here are three helpful ideas.

1. The advantage of a phone call is that the person you're calling can't see you, and if you blow it, they never will. What have you got to lose?

    If you feel you just failed with a very good prospect, call her back, or write her a handwritten note, admitting your bumbling effort. "I'm terribly sorry for wasting your time, Ms. Merriweather. I'm not sure what happened, but I truly believe we have an excellent product fit. With your permission, I'd like to start over." Who can resist such honesty?

2. Approach it as if it were a *personal* business call, rather than a *career* business call. Most of your professional business can be handled the same way as you would take care of your personal business.

3. Approach your calls as if you were the buyer. Develop and use a buyer's mentality. **You're in charge**. Your voice should sound confident.

OPEN

"Hello. This is Sarah Johnson. I have a '95 Corolla and I'd like to trade it in for a '98 sports utility vehicle. Naturally, I'd like a good deal."

HOOK

"Price may not be a primary factor in this deal. Service is very important to me. I'd like to see what you have for me to look at."

CLOSE

"I'm only available to meet in the evening. I can meet this Thursday or Friday."

You, as the buyer, have the upper hand. The seller is obviously going to accommodate money walking through the door. Assume a buyer's attitude.

Ask for referrals from everyone you can think of.

Ask your dentist where he buys his shoes, your mother-in-law where she buys her plants, your kids who makes the best pizza. Ask your boss for the name of his favorite restaurant. Ask the waiter at the restaurant where he eats dinner. Never stop asking. These are good things to know, even if you're not selling. Selling gives you an excuse to be nosy.

Developing a client list is a legitimate way of meeting new people. It beats hanging out in bars and asking a person her astrological sign. You can put yourself on the line without humiliating yourself or taking a personal risk. It could be an encounter that goes nowhere without loss, or it could be the first of many meetings that may be mutually beneficial. *There is no downside.* **Pick up the phone.**

CHAPTER FOURTEEN

Your First Meeting

This is no blind date. This is no set up. You know something
about the person you're going to see. You've initiated the meeting.
You have control over the meeting and you are prepared
to take it to the next step. This is no occasion for sweaty palms.

OLLOWING UP ON THAT, don't underestimate the value of a good handshake. Your handshake is your first contact. It establishes two things about you:

1. **Your handshake is a measure of appropriate self-esteem.** Think of the story of The Three Bears. Papa Bear is too hard, carrying too much bluster, grabbing for control. Mama Bear is too soft, giving a feeling of hesitancy and deference. I don't know about Baby Bear. But I like Goldilocks. She walks right in, assesses the room, considers her options, and settles on "just right." Curious, but no daredevil; cautious, but not afraid. She has a straightforward handshake, brief, firm, and hearty.

2. **Your handshake indicates your intention to do business.** It sets the tone of your demeanor. Make sure it represents you well.

The most important word in any language is a person's name.

+ Use your client's name often. Help your client to use your name. Get her name and title clearly input into your consciousness as soon as you can.

+ Some people use mnemonic devices to help people remember their names. One person who worked with me used mnemonic devices that were quite memorable. When he handed someone his business card he said, "Name's John Cheshier. John as in toilet; Cheshier as in cat." Got a picture of that? Are you apt to forget his name?

     Learn to use mnemonic devices, to help you remember people's names. I attended a seminar that focused solely on increasing memory capacity through the use of mnemonic devices. (Burly Shirley/Curly Shirley/Surly Shirley/Squirrelly Shirley. Since I'm neither burly nor curly, I guess it's surly or squirrelly.)

+ Exchange cards *at the beginning* of the meeting, so you may use each other's names during the meeting. It's also useful in case there is a need for further introductions either during the meeting or immediately following the meeting.

+ Using names helps to establish a comfort level from the beginning. It also helps to keep you *specifically* top of mind, after the meeting is over and you have left the premises. Buyers meet new people every day. It is your intention to be remembered. Knowing your name helps them to remember you.

+ You will meet people again, in other settings. Being able to remember a name gives you the opportunity to greet them by name. This will make them feel important personally, and look important to whomever they are with.

Where the meeting takes place sets the tone of how the meeting will be conducted.

The meeting is in their office:

✦ Don't sit until you are invited to. Then sit so you can establish a good, level eye contact with them. Look your client right in the eye. No one likes shifty eyes.

✦ Sit close enough to see and hear your client clearly, and close enough to share written material, should it materialize.

✦ If you are shown a chair that's too far away, and if the chair is easy to move, ask for permission to move it where you want it. Put it back when the meeting is over.

✦ If the chair is not movable, sit on the front half of the seat and lean forward. The person you are speaking to more than likely will mirror your action and also lean forward, making her attention easier to capture.

The meeting is in your office:

✦ Greet your guests in the reception area. "Send them on back," when they have not been to your office before, is rude.

✦ Lead the way. You know it; they don't. If they get ahead of you, give them instructions before the turns.

✦ Invite them to sit down, and motion toward the place where you want them to sit. Allow them the same courtesy you would ideally want for yourself, i.e., comfortable chairs near the place you will be sitting.

In either office, the formality of the meeting is your call.

✦ If your client is behind a desk, get as close to the desk as you can so you may use their desk for your presentation materials. If the desk is cluttered, ask permission to put your materials on top of what's on the desk, or to move it off the desk.

✦ If you are behind a desk and you want the power, lean forward, put your forearms on the table and ask your guest to begin.

✦ If you are behind a desk and you want to establish a rapport, lean back, open your arms, and ask him how his weekend was, or something equally casual.

✦ If you want equality, sit someplace other than behind desks. Offices are being designed to accommodate seating areas away from the desk, for the purpose of equanimity. In addition to balancing the power, moving away from the desk gives the person holding the meeting the opportunity to establish the formality of the discussion.

The meeting is at a neutral site:

Food and beverage can relax the atmosphere and divert attention from the pressure of holding a meeting. When you set the appointment, ask the prospect if he or she has a preference for meeting sites. If he doesn't, suggest someplace off-premise.

✦ **Coffee shop**, for mid-morning coffee, is the simplest and least threatening place to have a meeting outside your offices, unless you're in Seattle, where having coffee has become an annoying native ritual. If you are in Seattle, and a native and an espresso freak, allow the other person and yourself a regular cup of coffee. What's it gonna hurt? Buying a person a cup of coffee puts no one in an obligatory situation.

✦ **Breakfasts** have become a preferred way to meet away from the office. Neither party gets trapped in the office first. The opportunity for being late is reduced. Breakfast takes less time out of your business day; breakfasts occur in informal places; breakfasts are cheaper than lunch or dinner. *Don't make it too* *early and don't stay too long.* Starting time is one-half hour to one hour before the start of the regular business day. Breakfasts may extend into the office business day for up to one-half hour.

✦ **Lunches** can be formal or informal. Don't get too fancy the first time out. Save fancy stuff for celebrations.

✦ **Dinners** are out, until you know each other well.

✦ **Entertainment venues** should also wait until a relationship has been established. At your first meeting you don't know if there is going to be a relationship. Sporting events and concerts are not throwaways.

If you are getting together at a place other than your offices, arrange to meet in a reception area first. Do not go ahead and be seated, and do not suggest that they do so. You want control of the seating, and you do not want the meeting to start before everyone is present.

Sit across from your client or clients, not beside them. Touching thighs is not a good beginning. Neither is sideways eye contact.

Keep in mind that your initial behavior sets the standard for your self-assurance and maturity, which translates into your ability to handle their money. If you cannot control a meeting, they will wonder if you can control their investment in you.

A *few ground rules:*

1. Bring only the essentials into the meeting room. That means yourself and your notebook, and a small amount of informational material about your company. This is not the time to roll out a performance. The first meeting is all about the client.

2. If possible, leave your coat and umbrella in an anteroom, or in your car. It's not your place to clutter up another person's office.

3. No profanity, smoking, or chewing gum.

4. Enjoy yourself. This is what you've chosen to do for a living, and it's just starting to get fun.

The Purpose of the First Meeting

The purpose of the first meeting is threefold: **Get to know the client. Get specific information that is actionable. Get an assignment to continue**.

There are several ways to **get to know the client**. After you've met the client you will be surprised by how little you learned over the telephone. Very few people look the way they sound. Just for fun and for the purpose of giving yourself an occasional jolt of humility, write a description of the person just after you've hung up the phone. Draw a little sketch. Write down a word or two to describe his office.

Get the first impression through his **mirror image**. What does he really look like, physically? How is he dressed and how does he carry himself?

Hopefully, you will meet in his office. A person's office reveals much about his position with the company. If his office is located in the middle of the steno pool, he is cast with the job department rather than the career department. If his office is located in or near the upper management wing, more than 10' by 12', and has at least one window, he's an important person and can make decisions on his own, backed by company approval. He's in the career department and he has authority.

If the art in his office matches the art in the reception area and halls, the company determines office décor and style. If the art appears different, he has been allowed to personalize his office and you can get an impression of his interests and creativity. If there is nothing on the walls, he probably doesn't like working there and has no intention of being there a long time. That may carry ramifications as to how seriously you accept his decisions and how much you may want to meet other people in the company.

You may comment on what you see. "Nice looking family." "Looks like you're a baseball fan." "So, you've met The President." Notice that these comments would indicate a response of more than one word, and more than likely will relax the client and get him to talk about something he likes or is proud of. Notice also that they do not offer an opinion, so you won't make a statement he could disagree with or dislike. "The President is doing a great job" may open a can of worms instead of a can a corn. (Baseball term. It means piece of cake, or easy as pie.) "Nice looking family" is pretty safe. I have yet to hear someone respond "Do you think so? I think they're ugly."

Ask four questions in every first meeting.

1. How did you choose to be in this business?

2. How long have you worked for (owned) this company?

3. How's business?

These questions will provoke a response that will let you know how they feel about their work and the company they work for, and they will build the bridge from the personal discussion to the business at hand, which is to **get specific information that is actionable**.

4. I'd like to ask you a few questions that will help me determine how I may be of help to you. Do you mind if I take notes?

You should have done your homework prior to your meeting so you may ask questions that demonstrate what you've learned.

1. You've been in business for five years. Is that correct?

2. You have five locations. Is that the number you want?

3. Brown, Little & Associates is coming to town. Do you consider that company a competitor?

You'd like more information, directly from the client's mouth, that will determine a problem for you to solve or a need for you to fill. Questions should be set up in a sequence that allows you to meet your objective.

1   Who are your competitors?

2. What share of market do you have?

3. Are you satisfied with your share?

4. Do you see any threats to keeping or growing your share?

5. If there were one single obstacle or problem you'd like to overcome, what would it be?

6. Are there any others?

7. How have you solved problems in the past?

8. Were they effective solutions?

9. What would you change?

Now help your client find a fit with your product by asking questions that lead to compatibility. I can't draft these questions without knowledge of the products of the buyers and sellers. You're on your own.

To **get an assignment**, you will have drawn a conclusion that there is a product fit, through your question and answer session. It's possible that you won't be able to determine a need for continuing the relationship in the first meeting. You don't have to come to an immediate conclusion, but before you leave the meeting you should have a pretty good idea as to whether or not an assignment is warranted.

After you have received all the information you will need to approach the client's needs, tell the client three quick things about your product, without giving a product pitch. If there is such a natural fit that you are asked to present more, make sure you're prepared to state your case in more detail. But assuming the usual first meeting conclusion, give out the following information

1. My product is _____

2. My product does _____

3. My product point of difference is _____

If you believe there is a product fit, ask for an assignment.

"Mr. Hope, I believe I can help you with some of the problems you outlined in our conversation. I would enjoy working with you."
"What's the next step?"

CHAPTER FIFTEEN

Effective Presentations

You make presentations every day—successful ones—
but you probably don't call them presentations.

P EOPLE TEND TO TAKE THE WORD PRESENTATION to mean BIG DEAL. Some presentations are big deals, and some aren't. Presentations come in many forms:

Oral	Sit down	On the street corner
Written	Formal	In your car
Video	Informal	At home
Stand up	In the office	Etc.

Any time you do something to get a response from anyone, including yourself, you are making a presentation.

✦ When you put yourself together in front of your mirror, you are presenting to yourself. You are also preparing to present yourself to someone else.

✦ When you meet your family at breakfast, or your colleagues at work, you are presenting yourself. You are setting them up for who you are today. When you are smiling, it's okay to say "Hi." If you're frowning, people are on notice to watch their step.

✦ When you negotiate the price of a purchase at an automobile dealer or a garage sale, you are presenting.

✦ When you want a diamond ring for Christmas, you stage a series of presentations to make the sale.

✦ When you want a good score on your final exam, you present your answers in the best possible form of knowledge and persuasion.

✦ When you are going after that new job, you present yourself through your written resume. You stage a follow-up presentation in an oral interview.

It's a simple task to present to yourself, your family, your friends, and your colleagues. You are familiar with the product of yourself so you know exactly what kind of behavior you want to receive from them. You are the only one conscious of what you are doing and what you're going after. You set the tone, the time, and the parameters. Your audience is entirely at the mercy of your agenda. You are not unduly nervous. Since you are the only one who knows what you are up to, you can back out at any time and you don't have to explain your exit. It's your deal all the way.

What about when you present at someone else's request? What do you do when you don't know them so well, when *they* make the demands, set the tone, the time, and the parameters? How do you react when you know that you will be held accountable, win or lose? Scared as a jackrabbit pacing a pack of greyhounds? NAH!

Presentations done at the request of someone else should be just as easy as following your own lead. You initiated the original action and you've already gathered the information that will go into the presentation. The client, by giving you the information, has invited you to come and told you what he wants. All you have to do is give it to him.

The ability to obtain accounts and bring revenues to your company is more a result of your preparation and execution than the benefits and features of the product you are selling. Anyone who thinks that anyone can sell anything at anytime is mistaken. Products do not fly off the shelf by themselves. The fact that you have been given the assignment of making a presentation means that you have demonstrated an ability to do so.

There is only one reason to be afraid to make a presentation,
And that reason is lack of preparation.
And that reason is not acceptable.

Three key points:

Knowledge is power. Gather facts and get your knowledge in place.

You can't lose. You can only come out even or you can win. You go in with nothing. If you come out with nothing, you're even. If you go in with nothing, and you come out with an order, you win.

You don't need to win every time out.
In an average LP or CD, there is maybe one hit in twelve songs. That's 8 percent. The CD is still a success.

60 home runs in a single season is a baseball major league standard for excellence that has withstood the test of time. Professional baseball officially began on St. Patrick's Day, 1871. Until September, 1998, only two Major League Baseball players had hit as many as 60 home runs in a single season. All players dream of meeting that standard of excellence. Are the thousands of players who have not hit 60 home runs in one season failures? Not by a long shot.

Fortunately there are, and there always will be, more than one criteria for measuring success. You don't have to win every time out.

Rules for Preparing the Presentation

First Rule

There are no competitors. Not everyone agrees with me on this.

I believe that there is no need to muddy your presentation waters by including your competitors' names. Let them tell their own stories. Don't mention them unless you are asked for specific comparative information. Then you may respond orally. Don't leave behind unnecessary food for thought.

Second Rule

Be prepared. Know *your* product every which way...inside, outside, upside, downside. Know it so well you don't have to worry about it. But don't bore your clients with how much you know in one sitting. Tell them only what they need to help them make a decision about the presentation on the table. Don't take all your cookies out of the cookie jar at once. Save a little dessert for the next meal.

Be prepared. Learn as much as you possibly can about their product. You will be talking about and writing about them. A presentation is all about answering the client's needs with your benefits, but first you must know their needs.

Third Rule

Be specific. Do one presentation at a time. If you have been asked to present a holiday promotion, don't go into your pitch for an annual commitment. Stick to the subject that has been predetermined by the client.

Fourth Rule

Be flexible. If the rules change, you change. The client calls the shots. What if you've prepared an hour-long presentation and the client has had to squeeze in another meeting? If it cuts into your meeting 15 minutes or less, you should be able to handle it. This is not such a rare occurrence that you couldn't have a contingency plan to handle it.

To prepare for this possibility I put presentations together in segments, with some segments that could become leave-behinds. Research, for example, can be omitted from the oral presentation and left behind for further study.

If you have agreed to a full hour, and they take more than 15 minutes back, then reschedule the appointment to take place within three days of the original meeting time. They owe you that.

If the client says there will be three people present and there are twenty, stand up and project. If the reverse happens, sit down and become intimate.

If the parameters change from a holiday promotion to an annual commitment, get out your tablet. This is the time to test your product knowledge.

If the client has changed the rules, you

are one up. You get to call the next shot. Don't become flustered by changes. Use them to your advantage.

Fifth Rule

Be creative. Creativity doesn't require a big brass band, but a little music to underline a point of emphasis might create a memorable impression. A recorded message from the president of your company to the people in attendance would add an extra touch to the importance of this meeting.

If the presentation merits discussion, bring along a snack to separate the presentation from the discussion. Everyone brings bagels. Think of something else. Fruit and cheese plate?

Dress a little different from the crowd. Wear a blouse or a tie in the client's corporate colors and feign surprise at the coincidence. If it's a sports pitch, put on a cap. Don't ask the client to put on anything unusual, however. Not everyone is comfortable in a change of clothes.

Put the client's logo—the real McCoy—on the cover of the presentation, rather than yours.

Start off with a door prize. Ask the room what last year's sales percentage increase was, then get verification from the manager in attendance. Or, ask what the high score in the annual bowling tournament was. You can enlist the help of a sales assistant to come up with a question. It sets a partnership precedent.

If you think they can handle the Big

Brass Band, bring it on. The point is not to detract from the presentation, but to add a few personal touches to set you apart from your competitors.

Sixth Rule

Rehearse. If for no other reason, it requires you to have the presentation finished a day in advance. But there are other reasons. Rehearse to get the timing right, to check for errors, and to make sure you've not said too little or too much. Even one run through will stockpile confidence.

Seventh Rule

Be professional. Retain control. Follow the first six rules.

Elements of a Presentation

All presentations need to have a hard copy. Whether you read it, refer to it, or ignore it completely and just talk off the cuff, you will eventually leave the premises. How else will the folks back at your office know what you've said, and how will the people you've presented to remember all you said? A contract will have to be written. Make it a part of the presentation.

No matter how spectacular you are in your presentation skills, the people you leave behind will not remember everything you say. They may want to review certain elements of the presentation. In addition, they may want to include other people in the evaluation of your presentation. They aren't going to call you back, and they aren't going to present it from memory. There must be a leave-behind for the people you leave behind.

Every presentation, whether it's two pages or two hundred pages, has five basic elements. All the information you need to give is contained within these five elements.

1. **Cover Letter**:   The purpose of a cover letter is twofold: It establishes a rapport, and creates interest in the presentation. That's all.

Thank you, Mr. Green, for the time you've given me and for the opportunity to present. (one sentence, one paragraph)

The purpose of this presentation is to restate your needs as I understand them, and present a marketing plan to turn those needs into bottom-line results. (one-to-three sentences, one paragraph)

I believe my company (accept owner-ship responsibility) can answer your needs in a timely…. (one-to-three sentences, one paragraph)

I look forward to working with you. (one sentence, one paragraph)

Sincerely,

The cover letter sets the tone of the pre-sentation. Make it a cordial invitation to the main event.

2. **Parameters**:   Restate what the client has told you in your information- gathering meeting. List the points in the order to which you will respond. Look at the people you are pre-senting to after each point is stated and elicit an affirmative response. If the client has sent you a written RFP (Request for Proposal), insert it into your presentation, and follow it, step-by-step.

3. **Body**:   The body of the presentation contains your response to the client's needs. You will have one response for *each* client issue. The responses will follow the order

of the parameters.

Unless there are many parameters and intricate responses, two to five pages should be sufficient. Clients don't want novels. They want facts and an action plan.

Resist the urge to include unnecessary research to back up your claims of superiority. One or two salient points are all you need.

4. **Close**:   Summarize the reasons for them to buy.
Ask for the order.
Set up the next step.

5. **Contract**:   For Gawd's sake! Have a contract with you. Do you have *any idea* how many sellers don't carry contracts with them? It's just *unthinkable* to not have a contract ready to sign.

Top Ten Finishing Touches

1. Prepare and hand out a printed agenda.

2. If it's a team presentation, every person on the team should have a speaking role. Silent partners should also be invisible.

3. If you are presenting to more than three people, stand up.

4. Know your presentation. *Do not read it.*

5. Do not hand out the hard copy of your presentation until the presentation is over, unless it contains detailed information that needs to be discussed along the way. If that's the case, hand out one page at a time.

6. The best way to handle the problem of a large amount of detailed information is to use visual aids on a screen. Stand in front of the screen to keep attention focused on you and what you have to say.
   a) It keeps heads and eyes up and looking your way.
   b) It keeps you on track and keeps you from forgetting important items.

7. Pause after each point, allowing the client the opportunity to digest the information and ask questions. I prefer questions during the presentation as they relate to specific items rather than waiting until the end for all the questions. Questions seem to have more relevance, and therefore are more easily remembered, if they are asked at the point of reference. When given a chance to ask questions at each point of reference, the client is invited to participate in the presentation, continuing the give and take relationship established in your first meeting.

8. Subtly prompt for affirmation after each point. This takes practice. You want the heads to nod, but you don't want to be annoying.

9. Remember to thank them for their time and attention.

10. Learn how to say, "Let's do it!"

Being able to give excellent presentations is the sign of a professional who has "arrived." It shows you know your stuff, you have listened to the client needs. It illustrates that you know how to respond to the task at hand and you are not afraid to ask for enough money to deliver what the customer needs.

Excellent presentations exude confidence and maturity. Clients want to give their money to people who have these two qualities.

Develop your own professional style and use it consistently. Clients also want someone they can count on.

CHAPTER SIXTEEN

Profitable Persuasions

*"You can't always get what you want, but if you try
sometime, you find, you get what you need."*

Mick Jagger, Rolling Stones

YOU'VE GOT TO FIGURE that someone who can rock 'n roll
into his sixth decade with the passion of a teenager has
to have negotiated something with someone along the
way. My favorite definition of **negotiation** is "to move through,
around, or over in a satisfactory manner." Mick Jagger certainly
does that, to the delight of millions of fans. While I am a few
persons short of having a million fans, moving through,
around, and over in a satisfactory manner is one of my favorite
things to do.

Negotiations begin with an objection. The inexperienced salesperson considers an objection to be a refusal to buy, or at least a
major roadblock to completing the transaction. Quite the contrary.
Research has shown that presentations resulting in a sale have
58% more objections than unsuccessful presentations. Rather
than being roadblocks, objections actually clear the path to closing a sale. They give us a clue as to what the buyer is *really* thinking. The prepared professional seller welcomes objections. Throw
me an objection and nine times out of ten, I've got you right where
I want you. A 99-miles-per-hour fast ball, if you can hit it, flies off

the bat faster and farther than a 75-miles-per-hour change up. Let's go whack at some objections.

Following my natural inclination for bottom-lining, I believe there are only two kinds of objections: "**I want to think it over**," and "**No**."

"**I want to think it over**" is a stall. There are two specific reasons why a buyer wants to think it over.

1. The buyer is making a minor decision to not make a major decision. You're dealing with an *Anxious* buyer, a *Fake* buyer or a *Consensus* buyer. The only one you can't do anything with is the Fake buyer.

2. The buyer is interested, but not excited enough to buy. Perhaps it's an *Eager* buyer who hasn't heard the words "free tickets" yet, or a *Hired Hand* who needs more information.

It's up to the seller to discover the reason for the stall. Stalls are for horses. Don't get stuck there. Here are seven possible ways to get out of the stall and back onto the track.

1. Call their bluff: "Are you saying that to politely get rid of me, or is there a specific issue...?"

2. Take the blame: "Perhaps I haven't explained...."

3. Question: "Are you leaning against it or for it? "Why?"

4. Icebreaker: "Don't you wish your salespeople were as persistent as I am?"

5. Empathy: "I know how you feel. Why, just last week...."

6. Worst case: "If you decide not to do this...."

7. Best case: "If we decide to do this...."

These responses demonstrate the flexibility we have as sellers to work within our comfort zones and use our own style to bring about the results we are looking for. I encourage sellers to select one or two responses that fit them well, and use them often. But try a new twist once in a while just to enhance your repertoire of behaviors and expand the kinds of customers you can work with. Obviously, different buyers will respond to different responses.

My favorite is #1. It's a surprise response, and the element of surprise usually brings an immediate reaction. The more immediate the reaction, the more honest it is. But try them all. Discover which one works best for you.

Once you get the buyers out of the stall and back on track, you should have moved them into position for an attempt to close the stall.

"Have I answered all your questions?"

"Is there any reason why we can't put the order through today?"

"This is right for you. Let's do it."

If hesitation is still in the air, back off. Sales is a lifetime commitment. No need for you to rush forward. Put the ball in their court.

"Why don't I step outside for a few minutes while you talk this through." "I feel there is interest on your part. What would you like my next step to be?" "Would you do something for me? I'd like for you to ask me to come back and answer three new questions. How does Tuesday morning sound?"

"**No**" could mean a number of things, but it doesn't mean never. It's the fast ball daring you to find a way to hit it.

1. No may simply be a test to see if a) you *care* enough to continue or b) you're *good* enough to continue. The tone and demeanor of the buyer will help you determine which it is.

2. No may be a stall while the customer considers your order.

3. No may be an emotional response to having to make a decision.

4. No may mean you haven't given them enough information to make a decision.

5. No may mean you haven't given them the right information.

6. No may mean the customer doesn't understand the information.

7. No may mean you haven't given enough good reasons to buy.

8. No may mean you haven't presented the right idea ... yet.

9. No may mean the timing is not right.

If you examine the possible meanings of "No," you will see that "No" doesn't mean never. It means *try again*.

The word "No" offers a great opportunity. It separates the creative, interested seller from the order-taker, depending on how it is handled. Do not accept "No" as an answer. "No" is an opportunity for you because it will stop most other sellers. If you do not accept "No," you will eventually get the order, if only because others do not press on.

The seller must understand that objections are not personal, and that they may have nothing to do with the presentation itself. The seller's job is to overcome objections in a rational manner, with an eye and ear as to the *real* reasons for the objections. Then overcome them, one step at a time, and get back to focusing on the original reason you are there in the first place. You thought this client would benefit from your product and services.

There is no right or wrong way to **negotiate**, but there are certain truths:

1. *You must be negotiating something that both/all parties want.* If you are the only one that wants something to happen, you will not get what you want. This goes back to the first truth in sales:

You must find out what the customer wants before any sale will take place.

2. *Something specific has to happen.* Therefore, action must be taken. You are looking for *behavior* rather than attitude. Don't be fooled by *like*. Like is not an action. "I like that" is not what you are looking for.

3. *Negotiation is time bound.* Set a time for the action to take place. If it doesn't happen, regroup and develop a Plan B or move on to other projects.

4. *Negotiation involves a balance of power.* Power is emotional. Control yours and you will control theirs, and uncover the hot and cold buttons.

5. *There must be room to negotiate.* Unless you've been specifically told to, don't go in with your bottom line. And if you do, recognize that even bottom lines can change. Some buyers automatically say, "you only have one shot so make it your best one." If a buyer has a habit of doing this, call his bluff once in a while. Go in high and say "That is my bottom line." Don't allow him to think that your bottom line is always where he wants it to be.

6. *Never give unless you get!* Negotiation does not mean they get everything they want and you and your company get nothing you want. I am still astounded by how many sellers will approach their sales managers and say, "They simply will not pay the price we are asking." And then stare blankly or with disbelief when the sales manager responds, "Okay, we can lower the price. What are you going to take away if we do?"

7. *If you get what you want without negotiating, you've probably given too much.* Notice the word, probably. Time is an element in winning. If you've priced your product aggressively and you

find someone willing to pay it, take it. There's nothing wrong with a gimme once in awhile. You probably earned it on another day.

8. *People expect to negotiate.* Most good business people enjoy negotiation. Have fun with it.

Good negotiators will:

+ **Build trust**. This is not about war where one side loses. There has to be a basic understanding that both sides expect to win. Respect that. Always deliver what you say you will, and give up what you say you will. Let your word be a certainty.

+ **Gain commitment**. Let them know that you expect the same from them. You will gain commitment and respect by being a worthy negotiator. No one will commit to a wimp. It's human nature to control all the goodies if you are allowed to, but it's not as much fun as negotiating for them.

+ **Know their parameters going in**. I don't like setting a fixed bottom line, because that's where you will end up. If you determine a range, rather than a top and bottom, it's been my experience that you end up a little closer to the top. If you enter thinking *I can take anything in a range of $40,000 to $60,000,* rather than, *My bottom line is $40,000,* you're much more likely to end up closer to 60 than 40. If you're thinking 60, you're not going to settle for 40. Not on my team, you're not.

+ **Not be afraid to hold**. Holding is a signal that you don't believe they're taking your position seriously. In the game of give and take, the third round is a good time to make a definitive statement. It's the natural rhythm of the childhood game of "rock, paper, scissors." Ba-ba-BOOM. Match me at the third stake, if you can.

✦ **Recognize that not all concessions are equal**. The negotiating points are on the table. They've given you parameters and you've responded to them. Now, attempt to place a perceived value on each parameter on both sides of the table. It's like trading cards. I have Bob Gibson and Lou Brock. You have Lou Gehrig and Billy Martin. Everyone knows that Lou Brock is more valuable than Billy Martin. But no one knows that I got to meet Billy Martin in Oakland when I was a kid, and I've got nothing to show for it. He's more valuable to me than market value. If you have that information, you might snooker me out of Lou Brock. Lou Gehrig would round out my Yankees collection, but if my Bob Gibson is 1967, forget it. His performance in that World Series is my quintessential baseball experience. To get the Bob Gibson 1967 card away from me, you're going to have to come up with something real special. See how this works? Negotiation is a process of discovering personal values.

✦ **Not get greedy**. Have respect. Know when to quit. Go after what you want, not what you can get. When you get what you want, stop. Getting what you want is the point of the negotiation. If you grab a moment and lose the future, you've lost more than you've gained. There may be another round some day and you don't ever want to start out owing.

✦ **Control their emotions**. You are negotiating issues, not persons. Leave persons out of it. There is a strategy called "Go to the Balcony." It means step away. Remove yourself from a situation, literally if you have to, to gain perspective. If you lose control, you lose.

Finally.... an old story:

✦ **Find the 18th Camel**. A father had 17 camels and wanted to leave them to his three sons. He willed the eldest son 1/2, the middle son 1/3, and the youngest 1/9 of his camels. When the father died, the sons realized that 17 would not divide by 2, 3, or 9, and they asked a wise person for advice. The wise one GAVE the sons one of his camels. Now they had 18. The eldest son got nine (1/2), the middle son got six (1/3), and the youngest son got two camels (1/9), leaving one left over, which was returned to the wise one.

There is another solution. There always is. Can you uncover it? If you can, you can negotiate anything.

CHAPTER SEVENTEEN

At Your Service

Service begins the minute you decide a prospect is worthy
of becoming a client. It's service that sets up a sale
and service that keeps the sale going.

SERVICE SHOULD COME NATURALLY. That's why it's so important to pick a compatible company or client. Just like meeting a prospective beau, without sacrificing your personal ideals, you think of ways to please them. This is not an exercise in altruism. This is the "If I do this, then they'll do that" theory. If I do something to please them, they'll do something to please me. If I do something to make them angry, they'll do something to cause me distress, like not buy into what I'm selling.

According to some psychologists, a person is capable of experiencing only four basic emotions: **Glad, Sad, Mad, Fear**. Every feeling we experience is a variation on the intensity of one of these four emotions. Love is a special case of glad, hate is a special case of mad, sympathy is a special case of sad, and call reluctance is a special case of fear. At any given time we are glad, sad, mad, or scared, and the state we're in will govern our behavior at that time.

People sometimes spend money when they are sad or mad, but that's when they spend money on themselves. What sellers are looking for is a commitment to spend money when people are glad. That's when they spend money on you. **Your Goal is Glad.** This is going to be a relationship. Make sure you and the other person in the new relationship are glad it's happening.

The Four Stages of a Relationship

In the **first stage of a relationship** you are eager to learn all about the new person in your life. You ask questions because you want to know all about her. You listen carefully to her, looking for clues as to her feelings, because you want her to want you to know all about her.

In **the second stage of a relationship** you want her to know all about you, and you want her to want to know all about you.

In **the third stage of a relationship** you develop lasting impressions that will either bond you toward developing the relationship further, or turn you away to find and develop another relationship. In other words, it's time to fish or cut bait. I'm not suggesting that you force a hasty decision. When you begin a relationship, set up a written system to initiate a series of timely evaluations that will tell you whether the relationship is growing or not. In one month, we should be here, at two months, etc. You can be flexible, but don't waste time fooling yourself. You don't want to leave fruit too long on the vine. If a relationship is past its prime, let it go. It's better to meet again, and you *will* meet again, on good terms.

In **the fourth stage of a relationship** you acknowledge its lasting presence. This could be the most rewarding stage, or the most dangerous stage, depending on how you handle it.

Stage One

You've decided to initiate the call. You are not a reluctant caller. You are an eager caller. You are about to meet a new person and you want that person to want you to know more about her. She hasn't decided to call you, so she is not yet interested in you. Don't begin with a rush of information about yourself. Simply identify yourself and the reason *you are interested in her.* You service her by showing your interest. The more specific and personal the interest, the more apt she is to allow you to continue. You will have pushed her glad button.

Be sincere, honest, and enthusiastic in your approach. If you cannot find a reason to express all three of these feelings, you probably have no reason to call.

"Ms. Hathaway, I just heard that Linens 'n Things is having a fifth anniversary sale. Congratulations! Only a small percentage of businesses make it five years. You must be doing a lot of things right. I'd be interested in knowing more about what you've done to make your store so successful."

Why would Ms. Hathaway even consider sharing her secrets with you?

1. You've noticed something positive about her store - "Five years...."

2. You're glad for her—"Congratulations...."

3. You've set her apart from others—"Only a small percentage...."

4. You've given her credit for the success—"You must be doing things right...."

5. You're giving her the human opportunity to share—"I'd be interested in knowing...."

In less than one minute, you have covered five key points to establishing a relationship of Implied Service.

Stage Two

Immediately after being caught off guard by this one-minute praise session, Ms. Hathaway will be suspicious as to why you are saying these nice things. She doesn't know you yet.

> "You may wonder why I'm so interested in your business. I work for Good Business Systems, and we specialize in developing retail business systems for people like you, who may have reached a maturity point of looking to streamline your business operations. Our systems will free up time for you to devote to personal pleasures or to consider professional growth opportunities. Does having more time interest you?"

The first thing you did right in stage two was to *anticipate* the possibility of suspicion about your call. And while her suspicions that you may be a seller are correct, you managed that smoothly by going directly to product benefits that might interest her. You've added historical credibility to your implied service by saying you've helped other retail businesses. Then you offered a *specific area of service* that's pretty hard to resist. Who doesn't need more time? You've also offered attractive *results of service*. You've got her picturing two things she could do if she were to have more time: personal pleasures and/or professional growth.

The focus is still on this potential partner-to-be, but you've given her just enough information to get her thinking about how your service might be helpful to her. If she has not upgraded her systems to match her present success level, she will give you the opportunity to move into stage three. If the timing is not right, and that could only be if she has just recently upgraded, ask permission to send her materials about your company for future reference. *And* ask for a referral to other people who may be at the right stage for an upgrade in their business cycle.

Stage Three

We'll assume Ms. Hathaway is ready for stage three. Your timing is right, and your manner has led her to believe that you are truly interested in offering her a service that she can use.

In your meetings and resulting negotiations, you will see to it that Ms. Hathaway tells you what her needs are and how she likes to be serviced. The final negotiation should lay out what she expects from you and what you can deliver. It is very important that she understands two things:

1. You will do everything you say you'll do.

2. There are limits as to how much you can do.

Doing what you say you'll do should be a no-brainer. If you can't or won't do something, then don't say you *will* do it. Setting limits up front can be tricky, but you must do it. The way to do it is to go over everything you intend to do, and pause.

Look her in the eye and ask pleasantly, "Is there anything else you'd like for me to include in our agreement?"

If she says, "Yes there is. I'd like _____," and the request is reasonable, say, "Sure, no problem," and throw it in.

Is she says, "Yes there is. I'd like _____," and the request is significant, tell her you can do it for her at additional expense. Don't get yourself in the pickle of forking over money out of your pocket, asking the company for more money, or trying to hide additional expense under another category. And even more important, DON'T add additional hours to your service time.

If she says, "That should do it," take her at her word, but reaffirm.

"If that's everything, (slight pause), let's sign this agreement and become partners."

There are a couple of little things you can do to reinforce your commitment to her:

+ You can sign a pledge sheet. This is a personal guarantee, outside the company contract, guaranteeing your commitment to follow through on your promises.

+ You can draw up a pledge from your company support team that expresses the team's commitment to follow through with the agreement.

Stage Four

There are many things you can do to keep the relationship alive, so she will forsake all others while you remain involved.

+ Send her handwritten thank you notes from you and your management team.

+ Send her articles that pertain to her business.

+ Invite her to your place of business to meet the people working for her.

+ Periodically check in on how her business is doing. Ask her how the system is working. Ask her if there are any problems.

+ *Personally* handle any problems. Calmly explain what you will do and then do it. Don't dwell on the problem, and don't let little problems become big problems. Take care of problems quickly. Don't shuffle problems off to an assistant.

✦ If you have a need for what your client is selling, buy it from her. Partnerships work both ways.

✦ Some clients start out prickly and settle down after they're certain they've made a good deal. Give them time to get used to working with you and your product.

✦ Periodically surprise your client with tickets to a concert or dinner scrip. Take her to lunch yourself. Don't save all the attention for when renewal time comes up or you have a new product you want her to try.

✦ Get to know all the members of your client's team. They will help with any problems that may occur internally if they like you and your product. And you never know. Anyone can be promoted. One of the current team members may become the team leader some day.

✦ If the person you are working with intends to leave the company, ask her to introduce you to her replacement. When the new person is in place, send a small gift that will keep you top of mind, like a new appointment calendar with your name written on Monday of her third week, along with a message of congratulations.

✦ If the person you are working with leaves the company, stay in touch. If she's been a person in authority at one company, more than likely she will resurface at a similar level with another company. One of the first things a person does in a new job is contact the people she's worked with and liked in her previous job.

Always keep in mind that you are working with *people*, not companies.

Treat the people you work with the same as the people you live with.

If you can't do that, you are working with the wrong people. Move on.

CHAPTER EIGHTEEN

Projecting Your Income

*The term "Time is Money" is an axiom that applies directly
to commissioned sales. You may think you're not being paid
an hourly wage. Think again.*

A S A COMMISSIONED SELLER, I consistently keep track of my
time. Every minute I spend on the job holds the possibility of financial return for my family and me. As a
sales manager I am constantly amazed at how few sellers
understand this. As a sales consultant, I am even more amazed
to find out that very few commissioned sales people understand how their commission structure works, and very few
sales managers understand how to set up commission structures and compensation packages that will motivate their sellers. **People do what they are paid to do**. Understanding this
is the key to producing the results that both sales managers
and sellers want.

Studies on why people work and what they work for invariably
reveal that money ranks only fourth or fifth on the job satisfaction
scale. Working atmosphere, friendly people, doing what they like,
recognition, and other feel good items rank above money as reasons why people like their work. HOWEVER. This holds true *only*
if people are satisfied with their incomes. If they feel they are
earning the right amount of money for what they do, money is not

the most important issue for job satisfaction. If people feel they are underpaid, money moves to the top of the list.

How do you know if your are making the right amount of money for what you do? There are two ways: **Compare your income to others in like positions. Compare your income with your personal goal fulfillment.**

Before we look at how to determine if you are making as much money as you should, we'll examine what goes into determining the cost of labor.

The word *money* ranks right up there with the word seller on the tasteless discussion list. Well, get over it. We're going to use the word money a lot in this chapter. Unless someone comes up with a better way to reward performance and pay for food, housing, and new Porsches, money will have to suffice. And whether you want food and housing and no Porsches, or food and housing and Porsches, will determine where you decide to work and what you are willing to do to earn the money.

There are certain truths in the amount of money you will make as a commissioned sales person.

1. The percentage of commission you make is directly related to the unit price of the product you are selling.

     The reason for this is the assumption that it takes longer to sell a $100,000 item than a $10,000 item. To earn $2,000 commission for selling a $100,000 item, the commission rate is 2%. To earn $2,000 for selling a $10,000 item, the commission rate is 20%. Given our assumption, is this fair?

2. The percentage of commission you make is directly related to how many items the company projects to sell.
     a) If the company estimates it will sell fifty $100,000 items per year, the annual company income is $5,000,000.
     b) If it estimates the cost of seller commissions at 10%, it will budget $500,000 to pay its sellers.
     c) If it wants to cut expenses, it will allocate 5% to commissioned sales, and the budget is $250,000.

3. The percentage of commission you make is directly related to how difficult the product is to sell, and that is determined by consumer demand for the product and the level of competition in the product line.
   a) If the product is difficult to sell and the product has strong competitors, the company will pay more to get and keep better sellers.
   b) Sellers who make $100,000 a year are more motivated than sellers who make $50,000 a year.
   c) A budget of $500,000 will get a company five highly motivated sellers earning $100,000 per year.
   d) A budget of $250,000 will get a company five very good $50,000 per year sellers who will jump ship when their motivational needs accelerate.

4. The percentage of commission you make is directly related to how much other sellers who are selling the same or similar product as you sell are making.
   This goes back to item # 3. Industry surveys take place all the time. Employers know who's paying what. There are industry standards. Find out what that standard is for entry level and senior level sellers. Your interest is in what you will make not only this year, but also over the next five years.

5. Employers will pay as little as they can to get the kind of people they want. The less money they pay out, the more money they keep. No explanation needed. That's why they do surveys.

6. The higher the income, the higher the expectations on performance, the higher the level of on-the-job stress.
   Employers who pay a seller $100,000 a year want to make sure the seller maintains a certain level of sales.
   a) $100,000 commission @ 10% means the company expects to bill $1,000,000 from your efforts.
   b) They have $900,000 left after they pay you.
   c) If you don't make $100,000, they don't make $900,000.

Employers who pay their sellers $100,000 a year want to make sure they are being represented on a high quality level. The manner in which you represent the company is as important to them as the amount of product you sell. It's not either/or. It's both.

When you **compare your income to others in like positions**, you need to look at two things. Look at what people at other companies are making, and *all other things being equal*, the company paying the highest commissions moves into favored company status. But don't make a decision based solely on money, unless it's a HUGE income discrepancy and you make a conscious decision to sacrifice other benefits.

Look at what people at your favored company are *actually earning*. Opportunity is as important as commission rates.

1   If lower commissions are being paid for a better product that's easier to sell, does the commission rate compensate for a more difficult sell?

2. How many people are on the sales force, and are they excellent sellers? If the inventory is limited, too many sellers will lower the income per seller.

3. Does the company have a capable management team that will help you make more money?

4. Does the company have on-going training programs so you will be well trained as you begin your work, and able to maintain a competitive advantage as your work continues? Beware of promises on this point. All companies say they train their people. Very few do. Ask for specific training information. If the company does not have a good training program and the company appears to be otherwise attractive, you may have to invest in training yourself. Ongoing training is a wise investment.

5. Look at the company sales support systems. Three items are critical:
   a) Good looking, effective **collateral materials**. What you hand out is not only a reflection on the company, it is also a reflection on you personally.
   b) Effective **research** to back your claims. Creativity is one thing. Operating on a wing and a prayer is quite another, and it doesn't cut it in today's high-tech world. Research is available on everything. Make sure you have it or at least have access to it.
   c) An excellent **support staff** is absolutely necessary to conduct business on a sane level. This is the deal breaker. No support staff, no job.

All these points add up to giving you the potential to earn the level of income you expect to receive, and the level you've been promised in the job search process. Make sure the potential exists. If the potential is there, only you can prevent you from getting what you want.

Compare your income with your personal goal fulfillment. Okay, buster, you've set your goals. You are the one who decided what you want and you committed to a plan to get what you want. Now you have to compare what you want with the opportunities afforded you in an actual job/income situation. You have to plan your time so you can fulfill your commitment to yourself.

Start with a personal budget. *Oh how boring*, you think. I'll let the wife do it, or the big strong man of the house do it. Don't get lazy on me now. Commissioned sellers are *actively involved in setting personal budgets*. Your personal needs and desires have determined what your income goals will be. That's the difference between commissioned sales and an annual salary. Remember?

Let's work with $100,000. It's a nice round figure that makes for easy percentages. Well-run businesses plan budgets by percentages, rather than actualities.

Personal Budget

Based on annual gross income of $100,000

IRS, FICA, Unemployment comp., Medicare*	30%	$30,000
401K	10%	$10,000
Take home pay (net)	60%	$60,000
	GULP!	

Actual budget based on net pay

House payment	30%	$18,000
Utilities, etc.	3%	1,800
Automobile	12%	7,200
Home Food	12%	7,200
Restaurant Food	8%	4,800
Clothing	8%	4,800
Investments	10%	6,000
Emergency Fund	5%	3,000
Miscellaneous	4%	2,400
Travel and Entertainment	8%	4,800
	100%	$60,000

* I used standard tables from the IRS. With deductions, you could lower that amount and reclaim about $10,000.

The purpose of this exercise is to clarify exactly what you have to earn to live the way you want to live. One Hundred Thousand Dollars a year sounds awesome. It's about $8,400 a month. That sounds less awesome. It's about $1,925 a week. Practically nothing.

What is your hourly wage?
40 hours a week, times 52 weeks   =   2,080 hours
2,080 hours divided into $100,000   = $48 per hour
Your time is worth $48 per hour.

Time Allocation

No matter what you determine your income will be, it boils down to an hourly wage. The difference in a commissioned seller's hourly wage and a salaried employee's hourly wage, is that *the seller, rather than the employer, determines the hourly wage.* If making $100,000 dollars a year puts too much pressure on you, okay. Select a position that requires less output. If making $100,000 a year is not enough, that's okay too. Increase your output. *You decide.*

Here are the things a commissioned salesperson has to do:

1. Prospect for new business.

2. Make appointments.

3. Hold face-to-face meetings.

4. Prepare proposals.

5. Make presentations.

6. Service customers.

7. Upsell current accounts.

8. Plan and set goals.

9. Complete paperwork.

10. Make collections.

You have to do all of these things. People who fail don't do the things they don't like to do. People who succeed don't like to do the same things that people who fail don't like to do, but they do them. What does the successful person do that the unsuccessful person does not do?

1. The successful person focuses on results. It's the if/then theory. If I do this, then this will happen. Successful people count on

the result to be positive. The successful person has a positive, optimistic attitude.

2. The successful person is tactical in his allocation of time. He evaluates every minute. Begin your evaluation by writing down all the tasks of your job. Next, *place a dollar value on each task.* Then allocate your time according to the values you've assigned.

 Paperwork and face-to-face selling do not hold the same value. Let's give paperwork a $25 per hour value and assign face-to-face selling a $150 per hour value. That means you dedicate a ratio of one hour of paperwork to six hours of face-to-face selling.

3. The successful person is relentless in following his plan. That doesn't mean there are no time outs. Leave room for breathers. Schools require ten minutes per hour between classes. That's fair. Put ten minutes per hour in your plan. In an eight-hour workday that gives you forty minutes in the morning and forty minutes in the afternoon for unscheduled time, in addition to your lunch break.

 And speaking of lunch, you get no accolades from me for not taking lunch breaks. You're never too busy for lunch, only too stupid. Food for the belly is food for the mind as well. And proper digestion requires a relaxing atmosphere. Take time to find a nice place to eat and eat good food. Running on empty is an inefficient use of your time.

4. The successful person is open to new ideas and procedures. Aware of the fallacy of status quo, and understanding that there will always be someone trying to take his position and his money, the successful person keeps himself up to date on progressive techniques and fashions. He regularly comes up with new ideas to surprise and delight the people he's with. The lesson of Scheherazade is a valuable one that will keep the knock of obsolescence away from your door.

Successful people find a balance of discipline and enthusiasm that keeps them on track and motivated toward growth. The successful person has fun and is fun to be with. I am happier when I feel successful and when I'm in the company of people who also feel successful. How about you?

CHAPTER NINETEEN

What If You Lose?

*You can't win 'em all. What we do about our losses
determines how our lives are going to play themselves out.
Winners move forward, knowing that a loss is only a setback.
Losers get stuck on the loss.*

THIS BOOK IS ABOUT making sure your life is the best it can be by taking specific action to control what is happening to you. In that context, you can't lose. You may have setbacks, but you can control them. There are tragedies in this world, real tragedies like earthquakes that kill thousands of people, or a single child dying of leukemia. It's not my intention to make light of them, but that is not what this book is about. Having said that, let's move on to taking care of our setbacks.

We will start with the simplest of losses, the loss of a sale. The steps to overcoming this setback are the same steps, broadened, that will help you overcome more serious setbacks.

You Lose the Sale

You've given it your best shot. You gathered all the necessary information, you put together the best possible presentation, you asked for the close at the most opportune time, and you did not get the sale. What happened?

The first question to ask yourself: Is this loss important enough to investigate? The answer is yes. Every loss is important, so throw away that question. Every loss, to be sure, does not require the same amount of time to investigate, but you do need to know why a proposed sale did not go into the win column. Losses, even small losses, can sneak up on you, until you've gathered enough of them to seriously affect your income. You can lose your winning edge quickly by forgetting to cover one or two small details. It is important to understand the reasons for each loss.

The next question to ask yourself: Did you really give it your best shot? This is a tough question, because you have to be honest in your appraisal. One of the hazards of experience is skipping over the details. When you first start out in sales, you have your checklist, to make sure every base is covered. Now that you know it all and do it all automatically, everything is done the way it is supposed to be done. Or is it? Take out the checklist again and go over the basic details of selling.

1. *Did you really listen?* Or did you anticipate what you thought the client was going to say, because you've heard it all before? One time I put together a media buy for a car dealer, based on a demographic of Adult buyers, between the ages of 25 and 54, because dealers "always" ask for Adults 25-54. This particular car dealer actually said Women 25-54, but I didn't hear that. I was anticipating, rather than listening, and I missed the whole point of the ad campaign. I also missed the sale. Don't forget to listen to every word.

2. *Did you talk too much?* Did you get so far into telling your client all about your product that you forgot to leave time for him to talk about his product? Was your head too full of yourself to allow the customer his selling time? You must allow the customer time to speak first and most. The customer always gets the first word, the last word, and most of the words in between.

3. *Were you enthusiastic?* I've walked through tire warehouses and exclaimed over the great new x-1037-3 anti-skid model, when it looked to me to be exactly like the other 750 tires on the shelves around it. Did you forget the exclamation points this time out? That new account executive from your competitor's office probably is full of !!!'s.

4. *Did you underestimate the competition?* They are always there. If you usually get the buy, you can be sure they are trying harder to come up with newer ideas and more creative packaging and pricing to try to take away your money. If you have not yet made a sale with this company, you can be sure those who have all the marbles are defending their position, with gusto.

5. *Was your presentation really good?* Did you remember to thank him for his time and attention, to restate the parameters, to follow your outline, to notice his expressions along the way, to hear the close signals, etc., or did you slide over a point or two? You can't ever cut corners. You may have heard your presentations a thousand times, but each client knows only what you present to him or her. You may leave out an important detail if you make assumptions, or you may fail to notice his eyes glaze over as you plow through in your disinterested monotone.

6. *Is the buyer's product right for you and your product?* It could be that there really wasn't a fit there. Perhaps your benefits just don't suit the buyer's needs. Remember to target your efforts honestly to those that make sense for both of you. Save your efforts for those that count. Don't try to force what's not there.

7. *Did you do what you said you'd do?* We sometimes take our clients for granted, hoping they'll understand if we are busy and can't get back to them right away. Perhaps you didn't get the presentation done on time. Being late with presentations is the most common mistake salespeople make with familiar clients. Always perform exactly as you say you will, when you

say you will, even with, or *especially* with, people you know. They will be the most disappointed with a poor performance because they've come to expect more.

8. *Did you properly service this client the last time out?* No apologies accepted. If your service has been slow in the past, it will kill your chances of keeping the business, no matter how good a job you did with this current presentation. Past performances are the starting gate for every event.

9. *Are you answering these questions honestly and objectively?* Take the ego out. No one is looking over your shoulder. Answering these questions honestly and objectively can only help your business.

If you've answered these questions honestly, and you discover that you did miss a few details and you didn't do a good, complete job, what do you do about it? You confront it, of course. You never, never walk away from problems, or sink down into a corner, hoping you will never see this person again. Mark my word, you will encounter this person again, *especially* if you've blown it. These ghosts of business lost somehow creep into your business life again, usually in another position, at a higher level, in a larger company. Then you have to eat crow. I've eaten my share of crow. Better that it be a small meal.

You are going to call this person who just left you off his buy and say, "Charley, I'm sorry we are not going to be a part of your new product promotion. I was reviewing my notes on this, and I screwed up. I failed to thoroughly answer your questions about my product, and properly position the possibilities of our proposed partnership. I hope you will consider my company the next time out. Our companies should be working together."

Then stop talking and listen to Charley. No further lamentations or self-beatings. Make this simple statement to the client, acknowledging your acceptance of the responsibility for this not working out. That's not so bad, is it? If you address this now, you can walk up to Charley and shake his hand any time you meet him again.

It's quite possible that you, being the outstanding seller you are, have gone through the checklist and found no omissions and no absence of enthusiasm. You did everything right. Then what? Wait a few days and call the client.

There may have been something going on that you knew nothing about. The reasons for your not getting the sale may be more difficult to address because they have nothing to do with your performance. They may be personal or they may be confidential. Perhaps Charley's job was on the line for another reason and he didn't have time to carefully look over all the presentations. Perhaps Charley's dog was run over by a car the morning of your presentation and he couldn't concentrate on what you were saying, so he selected the previous day's best pitch. This actually happened to me. Perhaps Charley's manager's father-in-law owns your competitor's company.

If you know Charley well, wait a few days and give him a call. Tell him you are confused as to why your company (not you), did not get this particular contract. Charley will probably tell you the truth. If he doesn't, then drop it and wait for next time.

If you do not know Charley well, or you know him to be extremely sensitive when his decisions are challenged, send him a note to allow him to view your objections privately. Hand write the note, if possible, and keep it informal. And do call him.

"I was just reviewing the parameters of the last negotiations we had. It didn't quite come together. I'm not sure what happened. When you have the time, I'd like to discuss it with you. I'll call you next week to set up a time to talk about it. Thanks for your consideration."

If you follow through on the sale, even if you don't get the order, then you haven't lost the sale. You have opened the door to the next opportunity, and now they owe you one. You have accepted the responsibility for this sale not coming together, and you have asked them for help. You are now in a much stronger position than you were before this whole thing came up. Looking at it from this perspective, you have just scored yourself a win.

You Lose Your Job

After you lose your job it's tough to do anything about it, except to find out why it happened, so it won't happen to you again. Perhaps you made a mistake. Companies should be able to handle one or two mistakes made by an employee, even if they are big mistakes, unless both mistakes were identical. Then the company may assume that you will do it to them again, and they don't want to take a third strike. However, the reason for losing your job usually is not anything as simple as making a mistake. Let's consider reasons more subtle than mistakes, to find out why you've lost your job.

The simplest way to find out why you lost your job is to ask the person who fired you. You have the right to know. If you are not told the reasons for your dismissal in the process of the termination ("it's not working out" is not an acceptable reason), then you not only have the right to ask why, you have a right to see your personnel file. There should be a written record of the reasons for your termination.

If you have been told why you lost your job and their records are in order, let's explore the possible reasons for your losing your job, and determine if they are valid reasons. If they are valid, perhaps knowing what they are will help you to overcome your personally harmful behavior before you get too deep into your next job.

Here are a few possible reasons for your losing your job.

1. *There was no job description.* Therefore, you never had a clear understanding of what it was you were supposed to do. Shame on you. Never accept a position working for someone else that does not give you a clearly written job description that both you

and your supervisor sign. Ask for a copy of the job description when you are considering employment, and keep a copy of it. You can not be held accountable for doing a good job unless you know what the job is. Without knowing, you leave yourself wide open for subjective evaluations and possible termination.

2. *There are no regularly scheduled evaluations.* First, you have to know what you are expected to do, then you need to be evaluated by your supervisor on a consistent basis, to make sure you are performing your job the way the company wants you to. I've seen many people lose their jobs, even though they were working hard, because they were not working hard on things they were hired to do. This is a bitter pill. You need to have written progress reports, signed by you and your supervisor, to make sure all along that you are doing what the company expects of you.

3. *You were not performing at a high enough level to keep your job.* Sellers should have written projections as to what the billing expectations are, in terms of hard-core results. One of the advantages of working in a sales position is that you know how you are doing. You either produce, or you don't. The results are in your billing figures. Because of this, you should know whether or not you are performing up to the standards expected of you. If you are not, ask for help before it's too late. If you are not meeting your projections, and you can't figure out why, and you don't receive help from your manager, start looking for another job before your self-esteem takes a tumble. Not every road to success is straight and smooth. You need help to stay out of the potholes. That's what managers are for.

4. *You could not get along with the people you work with.* I'm surprised at how often this happens. You don't have to like every person you work with. All you have to do is get along with them during work hours. If you are having personality problems with people at work, step back and see if you can get your

work done in a manner that does not involve interaction with the personalities you clash with. How far you can step back and whether it's you or the other person who makes the adjustment will depend on who you are and who they are. Pecking orders do exist.

If your problems are with a member of the support staff, you hold the edge, but be careful. Bosses are very sensitive as to how their support people are treated. Holding the edge gives you the opportunity to be more understanding. Don't be in a hurry to challenge the abilities of the support staff. Poor performance will be noticed and will take care of itself.

If your problems are with a colleague of equal job status, try to work it out between the two of you. Suggest a place outside the office where you can talk privately, without office pressure and interruptions getting in the way. If the two of you cannot handle the problem yourselves, go to your supervisor. If your complaints carry equal weight, seniority prevails.

If your problems are with your supervisor, you still have options. The first option is to meet the problem in a forthright manner. Ask for a private discussion. Keep in mind that the person may have a side to the story, and be open to the other point of view. The important thing here is to ask for the discussion at the first signs of trouble, before it has time to escalate into a win/lose situation, with you being the loser.

Get right to the point of the meeting. "You seem to be displeased with my performance. Is there something I can do to improve the situation?"

If the difficulty persists after you have made attempts to change it, then speak with your Human Resources department. Again, try to accept at least some of the responsibility for the problem, but make it clear that you have been trying to solve the problem. You won't be told this, but it could be that you are not the only person who has had problems with this person. By going to personnel, you have at least established the fact that you are aware of a problem and you are trying to correct it. If you enjoy working for the company, but not for a particular person, there may be another placement for you in the company

5. *There may have been client complaints.* You should have been notified of each and every complaint, at the time of the complaint. If not, that doesn't let you off the hook, but it does give you cause for being miffed, for whatever good that may do you. If the client's complaints are valid, throw in the towel, and start fresh in another city, having learned that you cannot mistreat clients. One of them may be wrong, but more than one and you are the one who is wrong.

There could be a number of other reasons why you lost your job. In sales, if you are pulling your weight, losing your job won't be due to staff cutbacks. Whatever the reason, once you've lost it, your only recourse is to fully understand why. If it was due to company failures and inconsistencies, you've learned to investigate your employer more thoroughly, and to get the promises and expectations in writing. If you were terminated for reasons that land in your lap, hunch your shoulders and admit them, even to yourself. You are entitled to make mistakes, even big ones, once. Learn by them, and don't make the same mistakes again.

Your Loss Is Personal

A close friend of mine, Penny Smith, is a true working professional. She passed on marriage and children, and at age 41, was well on her way up the GTE corporate ladder. At 1:45 p.m., July 12, 1990, Penny received a phone call at work, telling her she had received the promotion she had worked very hard to get. She walked into her manager's office and accepted the new position, feeling very good about her life. A lifetime of working hard was paying off for Penny, in handsome rewards. She returned to her desk smiling.

The telephone rang again. It was her doctor this time, telling her that her routine mammogram had shown deposits that would require a closer look. He asked her to come to his office within the week for further tests.

Fifteen minutes separated the two phone calls, only fifteen minutes from having it all to facing the possibility of losing it all. What happens to a successful workaholic when she suddenly learns that there may be something more valuable to her than work?

Fortunately, Penny has had a long-term career in sales-related positions and has learned how to handle the setbacks. She revisited her priorities and confronted them in a professional manner. Staying alive moved to the top of her priority list. All else became secondary.

Her first step was to get professional help. She gathered all the written information she could get her hands on, and interviewed several health specialists. She was given a list of other women who had had breast cancer, and she contacted them. Then she set up her personal support group and asked for help. Penny has been a one-woman support group herself all her life, so she was in a comfortable position to ask for help when she needed it. That's the way fully integrated life is supposed to work. We are supposed to be a community of individuals, giving and receiving goods and services from each other every day, in both our professional and personal lives.

When it came time for Penny Smith to receive the results of her tests, she was ready. She could hear the words, "Penny, you have cancer," knowing she had done everything possible to meet the challenge of fighting the disease, not alone, but with a host of resources to help her. Penny's cancer was discovered in the very early stages of the disease. She had choices in what to do about it. She could either have a mastectomy with reconstruction, a mastectomy without reconstruction, or chemotherapy without a mastectomy.

Without the mastectomy, there would be a 5-10% chance of recurrence. Recurrence almost always means a spread of the cancer cells to other parts of the body. Still, Penny was looking at better than a 90% chance full recovery, and not having to lose a breast. A mastectomy would give her a 100% chance of recovering to live a full life. 95% or 100%. It's not much of a difference. But the difference is life, and Penny has always chosen to live life at the 100% level. She saw no need to change her value structure at this point. She chose a mastectomy with reconstruction.

Penny Smith the workhorse would have taken off just enough work time to insure herself a full physical recovery. The new Penny Smith took enough time to make sure of her emotional recovery as well. During her recovery time, she visited a friend who was seriously ill with AIDS. On an impulse, she dressed as a clown, using what makeup and clothes she had on hand. When her friend saw her, he laughed. For the first time in many months, Penny heard her friend laugh, and she laughed too.

When there is a need, there usually is an answer to the need. Penny found a school that trains people to be clowns, and she enrolled. Now she is a part-time clown - a real, frizzy-haired, outrageously outfitted, goofy makeup, 100% clown. She appears at hospitals and parties as "Smitty the Clown."

Not long after Penny's turn of events, I was having dinner with her and her family. There were a couple of kids with us, and more kids at other tables. They were getting restless, so Penny reached into her bag and took out a red clown nose and a balloon pump and a bag of balloons. She began making balloon animals, wearing her clown nose. The kids love it and simmered down immediately.

Penny's brother watched her for several minutes and finally asked, "What's with the clown bit?"

"I had breast cancer," she responded. "It changes your perspective."

This is the same Penny Smith who, only a few months earlier, was placing nearly all of her time and energies into her corporate climb. Then, fifteen minutes after she had her hand on the top rung of the ladder, the telephone rang and the climb took on a new perspective. How would you have handled those fifteen minutes? What will you do when the ladder you're climbing gets kicked out from under you? Penny didn't lose a sale, nor did she lose her job. Penny lost a part of her body, and could have lost her life. Consider Penny's loss and take another look at what's happening to you. How do you measure your losses?

John F. Kennedy failed in his first attempt to get on the presidential ballot in 1956. We remember him, not for losing in 1956, but for winning in 1960. John Kennedy was the 35th President of the United States of America. Do we remember his "Bay of Pigs" fiasco, or do we still hear the ringing sounds of his inaugural address? He couldn't get a single piece of significant social legislation passed through congress, but we think of him as moving us toward new frontiers. John Kennedy moved past his losses. He was a winner.

In baseball, any player who can step up to the batter's box, take a swing, and get on base one out of three tries is usually called the Major League Batting Champion. He doesn't even have to score a run to get the title. He only has to reach first base. How about you? Can you at least get on base (make an appointment) one out of three tries? If so, you are a champion. One out of four tries keeps you in the major leagues. That's only 25% in the win column, and you're still major league. Who's going to call that a 75% loss? No one who's in this game for the long haul.

If you're batting 100%, you're not winning. You're playing not to lose. If you're not losing, you're not growing. If you're not growing, you're not living.

You are not going to win every time out. Accept that, and get over it. Lose a sale? Go after another one. Lose your job? Go get another one. Suffer a personal loss? Turn it around.

As long as we live, there is no such thing as a permanent win or a permanent loss. We will always have the opportunity to win and lose, and win again. Let's grab on to a new attitude about our losses and gain a new perspective on our lives. We're going to step up to the plate and take another swing. We're going to get out there and win at least one more time.

CHAPTER TWENTY

Keep Your Eye on the Ball and the Road Straight Ahead

"There are a lot more ways to get where you want and be what you want than people will tell you. On the odd road to success, it is not the vehicle that matters most. It is the driver."

Christopher Mathews, columnist

WHAT I LIKE MOST ABOUT THAT QUOTE is the phrase "odd road to success." It is an odd road. The author of the quote was writing about Irving Berlin, America's premier musical composer, who couldn't read or write a note of music, and Jimmy Carter, who got himself elected President of the United States of America by advertising his lack of credentials for the job, and Bette Davis, who couldn't have looked less like a movie star when she began her quest for stardom.

When I was a senior in high school, I went home for lunch every day because I was so quiet I had no one to eat lunch with. I didn't mind eating alone. The people I enjoyed being with were older and no longer in school. And because they were older, I didn't say much around them either. I just listened and learned. Never, ever, would anyone have predicted a career in advertising sales for this quiet little wren. But I wasn't concerned about my future. I knew I wouldn't be in high school forever.

I told you about my first professional sale with the General Sales

181

Manager of KOMO Radio. What I didn't tell you was that the General Manager of the radio station was not so sure I was a good choice to join the sales team. He knew the position had already been offered and accepted, but he asked to see me before he signed off on the move.

"Kind of quiet for sales, aren't you?" he said.

That surprised me. I'd never thought of myself as quiet. I thought of myself as focused, and I didn't see that as a detriment.

"I observe and I listen," I said. "That'll get me at least as many sales as your other sellers."

It was his turn to be surprised. My response sounded like a challenge, and he'd never figured me to challenge his observations. He told me later he thought I would agree with him and change my demeanor. He's not the only person who's made that mistake.

"You'll make more money than you ever dreamed of," he said.

"I dream of making as much money as you do. What makes you think my dreams are less than yours?"

Well! Surprise turned to stunning reappraisal. I didn't intend to sound impudent. His comments made no sense to me and I responded with exactly what was in my head. I told it like it was, from my center of the world. Fortunately, he viewed my responses as a show of personal confidence and he signed off on the appointment with no further hesitancy.

Irving Berlin heard music, Bette Davis saw stardom, and Jimmy Carter simply said, "I want to be your president." Once they made up their minds as to what they wanted they just went after it.

I'm not suggesting that I'm in their league by any means, but we do share a common thread. **We seem to have an ability to assess our skills and talents and use them to focus on a positive future**.

Let's review some of the things we've learned about ourselves and put a positive spin on each assessment.

1. My Mirror Image indicates that I am: _____

Has this changed since your original assessment? Has small and timid become small and confident? Has big 'n mean become big 'n strong? Do you stand straighter? Do you smile more readily? Make my day. Answer yes to one or more questions along this line.

2. My most memorable physical characteristic is: _____

(I have red hair. I am 6'10" tall. I have great posture. I have a distinctive voice. I have one green eye and one blue eye.)

3. I have courage, commitment and empathy. In addition, I have one special Gut Check that gives me unique strength. It is:

_____

Everyone should have one specific trait or talent they know they can rely on when the chips are down. It could be a sense of humor that establishes perspective or the ability to gather and organize facts. It could be extraordinary stamina or the talent to visualize a finished project or an extraordinary sense of timing.

4. I have a tendency to: _____ , which sometimes gets in the way of my success. I will take specific steps to overcome this tendency:

1. _____

2. _____

3. _____

Ain't any of us perfect, Mildred, and we don't want to be. Our tendencies are usually just fine, in the right place and time. For instance, I'm a linear thinker. I have a tendency to be overly direct and go right to the crux of a situation. I'm not quiet because I'm shy. I'm quiet initially because I want to assess the room and remind myself to keep the kid gloves on until the room is used to my bare knuckles. Even though they sometimes get in the way of diplomatic solutions, I wouldn't and couldn't give up the bare knuckles permanently. That would take away a unique strength.

5. When my day is not a perfect day, this is what I do to make it better: _____

If you *anticipate* a less than perfect day, do something to remind yourself to maintain an even keel. Wear a red dress, wear a rubber band on your wrist and snap yourself if you falter, leave your door half way shut and dim the lights slightly. It's helpful to make your coping device something visible. Over time, others will notice and either help you out or stay out of your way.

If a less than perfect day *arrives unexpectedly*, take a time out. Eat protein—raisins, cheese crackers, Trail Snacks. Envision chocolate sundaes, think about s__ —never mind—you do that anyway, or close your door and play a computer game. Have a funny one handy. Develop a specific triggering device that you use consistently, so the calming effect takes place quickly.

6. I am not alone. I have four people I can count on for support and encouragement.
   They are:

   1. _____

   2. _____

   3. _____

   4. _____

7. This is how I celebrate success:

_____

Tootsie Pop anyone? It absolutely astonishes me that people think they have to wait for birthdays and holidays and planned vacations to celebrate. Treat yourself at least once a week. Which comes first, the success or the treat? The first time, it's the success. After that, I believe that anticipated treats whet the appetite for success. Anticipate success.

Alex Suryan, an eight-year-old shortstop, and I were attending a Seattle Mariners baseball game together. We were participating in a special "future" promotion. Toward the end of the game, I looked at Alex and said, "Alex, let's come to a *real* 2028 baseball game together."

Alex said, "We won't be able to sit together. I'll be playing or...I'll be thirty-eight, so I might be coaching."

There's no doubt about the future for this major-leaguer-to-be. But positive futures are not just for children. Alex is my grandson. Will I still be around and going to baseball games in the year 2028?

**Sell yourself on a positive future and you'll find
a way to get there.**

It's morning. The year is 2028. I open my eyes and contemplate the new adventures that will come on this day. I look through the window of opportunity and see no clouds in the sky. Alex and I are going to the ball park, but we won't be sitting together. It's going to be an excellent day. Our anticipated future has arrived.